The SAPP BROTHERS'
—— STORY ——

Tough Times, Teamwork, & Faith

*Russ & Ann – May God continue
to Bless you two & My Best
Wishes*

Lee A Sapp

BILL SAPP · LEE SAPP

Addicus Books
Omaha, Nebraska

An Addicus Nonfiction Book

ISBN 978-1886039-81-0

Cover design by Peri Poloni Gabriel, knockoutbooks.com
Cover photo of Sapps by Tim McCormick,
  Rick Billings Photography
Cover photo of Sapp Brothers in field with sign
  by Omaha World Herald

Library of Congress Cataloging-in-Publication Data
Sapp, Bill, 1932-
The Sapp brothers' story : tough times, teamwork, and faith /
Bill Sapp,
  Lee Sapp ; foreword by Tom Osborne.
    p. Cm.
  ISBN 978-1-886039-81-0 (alk. paper)
1. Sapp family. 2. Sapp, Bill, 1932- 3. Sapp, Lee, 1929- 4. Sapp, Bill, 1932—Family.
5. Sapp, Lee, 1929—Family. 6. Businessmen—Nebraska—Biogra-phy. 7.
  Automobile dealers—Nebraska—Biography. 8. Christian biog-raphy—Nebraska.
9. Nebraska—Biography. I. Sapp, Lee, 1929- II. Title.
  CT274.S27S27 2010
  929'.20973—dc22   2010031423

Addicus Books, Inc.
P.O. Box 45327
Omaha, Nebraska 68145
www.AddicusBooks.com

Contents

In loving memory of our parents,
Hurless and Emily Sapp, and
our brothers Ray and Dean

The Sapp brothers, left to right: Dean, Bill, Ray, and Lee

Foreword

Throughout the Midwest, "Sapp Bros." is a household name. I have had the privilege of knowing Lee Sapp for the past forty years and consider him a good friend. I also have known his brother Bill for some time and have enjoyed my association with him.

Growing up facing the hardships and challenges of the Great Depression, the four Sapp brothers learned the value of hard work and how to persevere in the face of adversity. That experience became the foundation for their success in numerous business enterprises over the last five decades.

In addition to their business acumen, the Sapps have always been people of faith, and their spiritual values have been apparent in both their business and personal lives. The theme of strong family life runs throughout the whole Sapp family.

Lee has always been a great family man and displayed a tremendous devotion to his wife Helene for more than fifty years. I was very impressed by Lee's consistent care for Helene even after she had Alzheimer's disease and no longer recognized him. He spent time with her every day, giving her personal care each afternoon and evening until the time she passed.

Lee talks extensively about his children, Lee Alan and his late daughter, Lori Ann. I know Lori Ann's unexpected death from cancer, prior to her mother's passing, affected Lee dramatically, but he is very strong and resilient. He has continued to operate his businesses even past the age of eighty.

Lee has been very devoted to athletics in the state of Nebraska and has been quite generous with the athletic programs at both the University of Nebraska-Omaha and the University of Nebraska-Lincoln. Lee formed a strong friendship with the late coach Bob Devaney when Bob first became the head football coach at the University of Nebraska in the 1960s. Lee also has a strong friendship with Don Leahy, who was the athletic director at the University of Nebraska-Omaha for many years. I admire Lee's loyalty to his friends. Once he decides someone is okay, he is your friend for life.

Bill Sapp has been very devoted to his faith and has been generous to various Christian causes. He and Lee have combined extraordinary business skill and hard work with a very strong spiritual component, which is something that those of us who know them admire greatly.

Anyone who appreciates what it takes to overcome difficult circumstances and rise to the top of the business world will find the Sapp brothers' story compelling.

Tom Osborne, Athletic Director
University of Nebraska, Lincoln

Part I

A Nebraska Childhood

Train up a child in the way he should go:
and when he is old, he will not depart from it.
                    —*Proverbs 22:6*

1

My Early Years: Lee Sapp

See, only God knows when you're going to be born. He controls it all. He wanted us born in our time and our mom and dad in theirs. My time was January 18, 1929, on a farm six miles southeast of Auburn, Nebraska. According to the midwife and the chicken scale, I weighed a hefty fourteen pounds two ounces. Now that was the year the Depression started real bad, and that's the year my dad went broke feeding cattle, so I don't suppose I was in that house more than a year or two. I honestly don't know how long we lived there because we moved around so often.

Back in those days, Auburn was just a small town, but Hurless and Emily Sapp wouldn't move from the farm into town because they didn't want their children growing up in a "big city."

Throughout my childhood our family moved around southeastern Nebraska, but the countryside always looked the same wherever we went—rolling farm land with rows of trees along the road and corn, wheat, oats, barley, or alfalfa in the fields. We weren't traveling on paved roads, either. We didn't have them in those days like we do now. On the farm, we just had dirt roads that turned to mud when it rained. The gravel roads in town were a little easier to drive on.

We moved about every March 1 until I was a senior in high school. It seemed like either the landlord didn't like my dad or all of us living in one house or maybe Dad wasn't farming right. I think the Depression was the main cause, though. Whatever house we were in, we were a close-knit family. Each house became a wonderful home, one that was full of love. There were seven of us kids altogether. My oldest sister, Irene, was eleven years old when Bill, the youngest, was born. There's only five years between us four boys, though. Ray's the oldest, then me, then Dean, then Bill.

Those names—the ones we came to be known by—look pretty common, but they don't tell the whole story. Mom had a creative flair, especially when it came to naming her children: Veloura Hubka Sapp, Zelma Isabelle Sapp, Irene Emily Sapp, LaRayne Homer Sapp, LeLon Hurless Sapp, Harold Dean Sapp, and William Darlo Sapp.

My brother Ray was originally named LaRayne, and that's what he was called most of his younger life until he got to high school. He started school very young, and he was only sixteen when he graduated. Because Ray was younger than the other boys, he also was shorter, so everybody started calling him Shorty. I called him Shorty, my brothers did, and all the kids at the high school did.

After high school, Ray went into the service as Shorty and LaRayne, and he came out as Ray. That name was on his uniform and everything. He changed his name all right, and he was Ray from then on. I have no idea how Mom took to him changing his name; she never said anything about it, and just called him Ray, like everyone else did.

I grew up with the name LeLon. My parents called me that, and so did my teachers, and everyone else. In my baby book, Morton is crossed out for my middle name. They changed it to Hurless after I was born. Maybe Morton was the name Dad wanted. I think Mother didn't really like Morton, so she talked Dad into putting his own name in there. I shortened my name to Lee during my time in the service just because it was easier.

The baby book my mother made for me is a treasure. Mother wrote down just about everything you could say about a child, from how I would try to say certain words, to my being a pretty good boy—mostly! She wrote that I was often the life of the party, but I never liked to do my chores!

To help our mother out, my oldest sister, Irene, kind of got assigned to Ray when he came along as the first boy. I was the second boy and so the next sister, Veloura, got assigned to me. When I was a baby, Veloura was probably eight or nine years old. She changed my diapers and put me to bed every night and took care of me. We spent a lot of time together, and she became my closest sister. When Dean arrived, my sister Zelma became responsible for him.

As we grew up, Zelma became probably the biggest tease of the bunch. She has always liked to kid people; I think it has something to do with being the youngest girl. Always joking with kids, you know. She'll pretend to give you something and then there may not be anything there. That kind of thing. A lot of us called her by her nickname, Zeke. There were five years between me and Zelma.

Unfortunately, by the time Billy came along, all of the sisters were spoken for, so he was on his own. I like to kid him about that to this day.

Overall, Mother and our sisters took very good care of us. One time, though, when I was an infant in a basket, Veloura accidentally put my basket too close to the potbelly stove. It started smoking but it never caught on fire. Lucky for all of us! Our sisters really became close with each other because they stayed in the nursery and did everything for us. They were a tremendous help to Mother and just wonderful, loving sisters to us.

Growing up, all of us brothers and sisters got along real well. The girls would come out and try to play ball with us brothers once in a while, even though they were older.

Veloura and Zelma attended what later became Peru State College; they became teachers in one-room country schools. Then they started dating and they didn't have as much time for us, but that was to be expected.

My brothers and I were sure ornery sometimes. We especially liked to play tricks on the fellas our sisters were dating. We didn't know the guys very well, so we didn't do much at first. But then, once they started coming around more often, we pulled a lot of pranks on them. One of our favorites was to let the air out of their tires when they weren't looking. Later on, we usually got to thinking that they were okay, so we'd leave them alone. We just wanted to make sure that we were going to have three wonderful brothers-in-law! And we got the job done!

We brothers might fight once in a while among ourselves. But if a neighbor or two showed up looking for trouble and there were sides to be taken, all of a sudden my brothers and I were together. There was no doubt about that. I remember the Higgins boys lived down the road a quarter of a mile, maybe a half mile. We were all good friends, but one day in grade school they came over and we got in a fight—Higgins against Sapps! I have no idea what that fight was about, but they left with their tails between their legs!

Growing up, Ray was my favorite brother, probably because he was the oldest boy. We did a lot of things together—church, work, chores, school. He even helped take care of me, in a sense. We became the best of friends. One time, though, when I was real small and Ray was sleeping on the floor, I stepped on his head, using it as a footstool to get up to kiss Dolly Dean who was on someone's lap. Dolly Dean was the nickname of my little brother who was just nineteen months younger than I. After we had grown up and he'd long gotten over being mad, I teased Ray, "You can't be very smart if you let me step on your head to go up and kiss Dean!" I loved my little brother Dean very much.

6

When Ray would go out on dates, Dad had a deadline for him to be back. When he was late, instead of going through the front door, he'd wake me up. I'd open the window on the second floor, let down a rope that was tied to the bed, and pull him up through the window. That way, Dad wouldn't know whether he came home late or not. Like I said, we were good friends.

I actually introduced Ray to his future wife. She and I rode to school together as kids, and she rode her bicycle down to see the whole Sapp family sometimes. One of those times she was over, Brother Ray was home from the Navy and asked me, "Who's that filly?" And I told him. He must have liked her because they started going together and ended up getting married.

It's good our family was strong and loving because times were tough during the Depression, and most folks felt it. It wasn't much fun moving each year because Dad got a job with the WPA, the Works Progress Administration, after he went broke feeding cattle. I heard that more than 3 million people were getting this financial help by 1936, but some of the farmers weren't suffering like we were.

If we got on the school bus, somebody would always yell, "Here come the WPA kids!"

This caused a lot of fights. To be named as a WPA guy meant you were on government welfare, and you were going to get made fun of. Now if you moved far enough away, there'd be a new bunch of kids who didn't know you, and the taunts would start all over again. Tell you the truth, though, in those days, plenty of kids' parents were on the WPA—maybe the kids just didn't know it.

I remember our neighbor Mr. Reinhard Bartels also worked for the WPA. It was at his house that I met Bus and Elva Gottula's son Eugene. He was visiting his cousin Don

Bartels. Eugene, Don, and I were six or seven years old at the time. This was the beginning of a lifelong friendship.

When we moved from farm to farm, it was usually within about a twenty-five-mile radius. From Filley, Nebraska, to Beatrice, it was just ten or fifteen miles. When I went to Virginia, Nebraska, that was a different direction, but it was all of twelve miles. Bill would know more about Diller and the distance because he was the only one at home at that time. He went to school there. That town was the farthest away and that was twenty-five miles.

O'Dell and Pawnee City would be the next two farthest away, I suppose.

We lived mostly in white, two-story farmhouses. Some home owners tried to make improvements to their houses—mostly using cheap paint to try to make them look better. The main thing most families had in common was being poor. Homes back then weren't built with any amenities. Most weren't insulated and the windowpanes were just thin glass. There was no way to keep heat in and cold out. You were either sweating from the heat of the potbelly stove inside or shivering from the cold coming in.

Feathers are very warm. We'd sleep on a very thin mattress with a feather bed three or four inches thick on top of it. Then we'd have another feather bed on top of us, as well. But in rural places where we lived, we got a lot of snow every winter. And if there was a real bad blizzard, the snow would come in through the windows, and we'd wake up in the morning with snow on top of our feather bed.

In the mornings, because the fire had just gotten started when we got up, it sure felt cold. We'd stand as close as we could to that potbelly stove to get dressed. On real cold days, it didn't take long to go to the bathroom in the outhouse out back!

To get through the winter, we would start cutting down trees for firewood at the end of the summer and continue until winter started. We'd pile it near the house so we could get it inside in a hurry. We had to make sure we had enough to get through the winter.

Getting all seven of us kids bathed at one time and having enough hot water for everybody was not easy. Of course, very, very few homes had running water then. We had to go out to the windmill and pump water to fill our pails and then carry them to the house. I saw my mother out there pumping water so many times that it made me feel bad.

In the wintertime, we had a cookstove with a reservoir on it. We'd haul the hot water out on the porch on Saturday night, get out the homemade soap, and take a bath in the tub. We couldn't fill the water too high in the tub or we'd run out of it before all the baths were taken. We boys used the same bath water, but we each had our own washcloth. The girls naturally took their bath at a different time than the boys did.

In the summertime, we'd put an elevated fifty-gallon barrel in the sun to heat. After a few hours, we'd take a coffee can, poke holes in it, and let the water run through it, so we could take a shower. We all used it.

Of all of the houses we lived in while I was growing up, I did have a favorite—the farmhouse near Beatrice. It had running water in it. That was the first time we had baths and showers and toilets. The year was 1943 and I was going to be a sophomore in high school. You know, it was a beautiful white house; it set well, and it was a caliber above, quite a bit above, what we'd had previously, because it had indoor plumbing.

As far as family dinners went, lots of times I was afraid there might not be enough food for me. If there was a bowl of mashed potatoes or another food I liked on the table, I ate as fast as I could, so I'd have a chance of getting seconds.

That's how I became such a fast eater, I think! For a treat, every third week or so we might get a nickel to buy an ice cream cone.

Looking back, I remember our family prayed a lot. When you're young, you probably don't think of your parents praying about all the hard times the family's going through. But as you get older, you know they are. My parents were praying about how to pay $2.50 a month to Sears and $5.00 to the landlord—more if we were renting the farmland—and still have enough left out of the $45.00 a month WPA check to buy food and clothes for us kids. Praying was just the natural thing to do at our house. We had to pray for everything because some of the time we didn't have anything. We always said grace before every meal.

My mother was an angel. She was a big-hearted, wonderful, kind lady. Mom gave us lots of hugs and compliments and fixed the best meals ever. And for each of our birthdays, she'd bake us a special cake or a pie. Everything she made was good...but those poppy-seed kolaches! Oh, my. Those Bohemian pastries were my favorite—and still are! Mother's maiden name was Emily Hubka—a good Bohemian name. She really knew what she was doing when she made her pastries—those kolaches!

Mother was a school teacher for a time. In fact she met my dad when she was studying at Peru State College, then Normal Training Teachers' College, to become a teacher. She taught at a county school until she married my dad in 1919.

My mom sure was a hard worker, a very hard worker. Looking back, I don't know how she did it all. She kept the house clean and swept, which was a big deal in itself because all seven of us kids were always coming in from the mud, the dirt, the dust, and the hay.

Mother did all of the cooking and washing, and then she'd help with the field work, too. She would help shock the wheat, shock the oats, haul the grain with a team of horses to the granary on the farm, and milk the cows. She even helped Dad harness horses. There wasn't anything she didn't help him with. She did a little bit of everything, but come to think of it, like a lot of women of her generation, she never did learn how to drive a car.

I would say that I take more after my mother than my dad. Even my sisters say how much like our mother I am. They tell me that all the time. They say I'm always giving things to people, just like Mother always did. They say I smile like her. It's a nice compliment. It makes me feel good.

Even though we didn't have much money, we kids had a lot of memorable experiences growing up. We had a sense of a big extended family, from my mother's side mostly. While we kids were growing up, our cousins would ride their bicycles four or five miles to come see us. And we loved going over to Grandma Hubka's place to eat, just like people enjoyed coming to our house to taste my mother's cooking. My grandmother made the best kolaches. My mother had a great teacher in the kitchen!

Holidays were always so much fun. Christmas was my favorite because it meant I was going to get a lot of food to eat! We never got a lot of presents, though. One year Grandpa Hubka made a little wagon for us. He filled it full of popcorn and put hog cracklings on top instead of butter. That was our Christmas present—for all seven of us. They just didn't have extra money to give us anything else. You know, though, we all held hands, and the way I remember it, I was very grateful. Looking back, I wonder whether the popcorn itself was really the treat or was it the fact that it was

Christmastime and I was with my family. To this day, I am not sure why it was so special, but it was.

Christmas wasn't the only fun holiday. In the summer, for a long time, we couldn't afford to buy fireworks for the Fourth of July, but sometimes we would go into these small towns to see fireworks displays.

In the first grade, most of the year I had to walk to the country school. I had a horse I could use in the winter. That horse could find its way home, even in a blizzard. There were times when the weather was really bad, and I would have to rely on my horse to get me home. There were a lot of severe storms back then—none of them seemed minor.

When I was small, I fell in love with each and every one of my teachers. And because we moved around so much, there were a lot of them. They always hated to see me go, and they'd cry and hug me, and that'd get me crying. I went back and saw some of them after I was older, and they still wouldn't do anything but cry. But I don't remember many of their names. I can remember a couple of the high school teachers' names, most likely because they were the ones who were chasing me around trying to hit me with a ruler!

Chances are they were chasing me because I'd done something ornery. I was always good at math and history and biology, but I never really cared to be on my best behavior, you know. I pulled girls' hair and they'd yell, and all that kind of stuff. We'd take some little bitty guy and just hang him on a hook. It was during World War II, and most of the men were in the service, so discipline was lax. When the war was over, then discipline came back into the school. I don't ever remember being sent to the principal's office or anything, though. I must have been good at being bad!

I can tell you that things were different on the home front, though. If we did something wrong, which boys always do, Dad would tell us to go pick out a stick. I never will forget one time Dean came in with a short little stick, and he got the worst beating of all. I always got a stick that was pretty good sized after that. And as far as Dad was concerned, you never did get too old for the stick. And he had a razor strap in case he really needed it.

Now the family discipline was not always up to my dad. Sometimes my older sisters would take the liberty of helping him out. My sisters would put dunce caps on us and sit each of us four boys in the four corners of the kitchen. Because Bill was the youngest, he was the most innocent. Sometimes they'd let him get off the chair quicker than the rest of us, but we were all there. Four Sapps with dunce caps on—I still kid the girls about that one.

It was just part of growing up, you know. I think it was good—good discipline. And it got us all ready for the service; all four of us brothers would go into the military to serve our country eventually.

My sisters were more musical than I was, but I did take up playing some kind of an instrument because a pretty girl was playing one, too. But that didn't last too long. I didn't get my first real girlfriend until the ninth grade when I was living near Filley. In those days we would go to a movie or a family deal or something like that on our dates. I know she liked me or she wouldn't have dated me, but dating back then wasn't like it is today. There was no physical affection, really. After I switched to Beatrice High School, I started dating a couple of different girls. One of them was a cheerleader; I do remember that. I only took one of them out at a time, though, of course.

I played a lot of sports, but the one I lettered in was basketball. Back then, it seemed like there weren't many real tall people, so it was okay for me, being short and all, to play in those days. My coach, Ken Willits, is still alive today. Over the years, he always said I was one of the fastest players he ever coached, so I suppose that's why I lettered in that sport. One day we traveled up to Omaha and played Boys Town. The Boys Town kids were a lot older, a lot bigger than we were. They beat the heck out of us that day!

My brothers were more into baseball than basketball, though. Ray, who was two years and seven months older than me, was shortstop on the school team. When I became a freshman, they made me shortstop and moved him to third baseman. These were small schools, though, so we didn't have too many more players than what it took to fill up the field.

Back then, most kids didn't play a lot of team sports until the tenth, eleventh, or twelfth grades. Then there was a lot of focus on basketball. Some of those little schools didn't even have football teams, or if they did, it was just an eight-man team. I think Bill played a little football; I was on a leave from the Navy one time and watched a football game he was playing in.

My brothers and I enjoyed playing games together while we were growing up. For fun, we played our own kind of ball. In fact, we played every game you could think of, but we did it with sticks and stones instead of the usual equipment. I do remember playing checkers with Bill, though, and that was fun.

Mom tried to make the games we played more fun by cutting strands of straw from the broom. She'd just take a pair of scissors and cut thirty-five to fifty straws out of the top and give each brother an even amount. And those broomstick straws were our money. We used our straws to gamble against each other when we played pitch or pinochle and just about every game there was to play around that time. As far as who won the games, I think it worked out pretty evenly, when all was said and done.

But it wasn't all fun and games. There were times when the fun got a bit out of hand. I remember one time when Bill was going down to the cellar and Brother Dean was mad at him. Dean threw a brick at Bill and hit him in the head. We had to take Bill to the hospital in Beatrice. The injury was accidental, but Dean did throw it at him. Dean just told Bill that everybody gets hit in the head with a brick when they're going down to the cellar.

One time, Dean and I decided to take off and go duck hunting in the fall. Because we were just over a year apart, he and I did a lot of things together. I'd say Dean was probably in the seventh grade, and I was probably in the eighth. Well, we couldn't believe our luck when we came across a bunch of ducks all just sitting there in the lake near our neighbor's house. When we came crawling up there to them, we couldn't figure out why these ducks didn't take off. But we thought we had something good to shoot, so we shot a few of them. Back then, Brother Dean was really skinny. He shot the gun, and it knocked him back about a foot! He wasn't upset, though, because he was so tickled to be shooting those ducks!

Well, later on that night, we got a visit from a very angry neighbor lady. She came up to our farm and accused us of shooting her pet ducks dead! She was such a sight to see, shaking her finger at us like that, that Dean and I actually hid behind Mom's skirt. The lady wanted to be paid for her ducks, and our parents made sure she got her money.

That following spring in Filley, I was working at a filling station when gas was only nine cents per gallon. I couldn't believe my eyes when that very same neighbor lady pulled in! Since I knew I had shot her ducks, I became real nervous and ended up overfilling her gas tank until gas ran all over everything. Then she asked me to check her tires. I couldn't help looking back at her while I was filling those tires up with air. In fact, I was so distracted by her that one of the tires I was filling blew up! She was so mad she started to chase me, so I took off running. Since I was just a kid, I didn't have too much trouble outrunning a lady in her forties. I ran behind a building where she couldn't find me. The station replaced the tire and took the cost out of my paycheck.

More fun and games were to be had with the telephone. Back then, the phone system wasn't very good. You could pick up the phone, and if the neighbor was using it, you were supposed to hang up. Now, you could listen to their conversation if you wanted to kill a little time, but everybody already knew nearly everybody else's business. I'd get on the phone, and I'd say, "Gertrude, you've been on the phone long enough." And she'd say, "That must be one of those Sapps!" Oh, you know, everybody did it.

Just for fun, sometimes my brothers and sisters and I would walk a mile and a half to Filley to see free movies in the summertime. You didn't have a choice of movies back then like you do nowadays; you just saw whatever they brought to town. Most of the movies we watched were westerns with Tom Mix and Roy Rogers—mostly cowboy movies. The nearest movie theater was in Beatrice, though, thirteen miles away. In Filley, they just showed them on white sheets or canvases stretched out across two poles outside. We'd sit on wooden benches to watch them. When they changed the film to put in another film, well, that stopped everything. Then my sisters Irene and Veloura would get up and sing songs, and one of them would play the guitar, until the next film started up.

When you grow up on a farm, your day begins at 6:00 A.M. You milk the cows, you feed the hogs, you get the horses ready and harnessed, and you head out to the field. That's the routine. All us kids helped out on the farm, starting from the time we were small. When we were five years old, we started milking the cows. Brother Dean and I helped put meat on the table. Dad gave us one shell for the shotgun and, with the help of our good dog and the traps we'd lay, we'd bring home a rabbit or a squirrel. Many times, rabbit and squirrel were the only meat we had on the table. On Sunday, though, they'd butcher a hen or a rooster, and we'd have roasted chicken with mashed potatoes and gravy and vegetables from Mother's garden.

At one time, I would say our family owned about eight head of horses, which was a fair number. We also had cows to milk and a bull to breed the cows so they would calve at least once a year. We kids helped pull the calves out. We'd raise the cattle and sell some of them at the Marysville, Kansas, livestock market and sell their milk, as well. Sometimes we'd go to an auction and pick up some extra cattle, if we had the money to do it.

Hardship and being without is the best thing that ever happened to the four of us Sapp brothers. I got brotherly overalls and clothes handed down to me, whether they fit or not. The clothes went from Ray to me to brother Dean who was a little younger than me and then to Bill. It was really tough for my folks to see this.

When Dean was going to be an eighth grader, and I was going to be a ninth grader, a neighbor said that he would feed the two of us, board us, and pay us twenty-five cents a day to work for him. The deal was that my dad would get twelve and a half cents, and we'd get twelve and a half cents per day for our labor. We took the deal and worked hard shocking the wheat and oat bundles, and then we'd stack the bundles on hay racks pulled by a team of horses and take them to the threshing machine. After that, we'd pull the wagon full of grain to the granary and scoop the grain into the granary. We worked a lot of long hours.

Well, the thing was, everybody was grateful for our work on the neighbor's farm. We didn't live that far from the folks, so Mom and Dad would come over and see us. But when payday came, Dad took his twelve and a half cents and then he took about six more cents because he needed the money. It was very difficult for us kids to understand that. We had an agreement, and we thought we'd get twelve and a half cents a day. Well, at that time I thought he was the meanest man in the world, but he wasn't by any stretch of the imagination. He just needed the money.

In the past I've told my managers many times when they thought they were not making enough money to start the day earlier and stay later. I also reminded them that my dad was making $45.00 a month on WPA. He owned a '28 Whippet car. He paid $5.00 a month on that Whippet, $2.50 a month to Sears Roebuck, and then bought clothes and food out of the rest. Actually, when we had cream and eggs, we'd take them to town on Saturday night, and that's what helped buy the groceries. That's the way most everybody lived then.

Living through those tough times back then, we learned the most important lessons we ever got. My first job off a farm was working at a filling station in Filley, Nebraska, when I was in the ninth grade. Dutch Albert was my boss, but he was also my friend, and I stayed at his house when I was working for him. They fed me and everything. I don't know what I made at that job, but it couldn't have been very much. But I liked working. I still do. It was there that I learned that you had to bring in more than you took out. And I learned how to treat customers nice and joke with them a little. I used to wipe their windows and all that kind of stuff. But the next year we moved out of Filley to a farm near Beatrice, so I had to quit the filling station job.

When we lived near Beatrice, I stayed at Veloura's house and worked for her and her husband, Glen, on their farm. Every chance us brothers would get to go to work for him we took. I worked for him throughout high school and even for a little while when I came back from the Navy. Oh, he would pay us, but he'd work us from 5:30 in the morning until 9:00 at night! We learned a lot from him, though. We learned that you've got to be up early, and you better be ahead of your competition, whatever kind of work you do. I always thank him for the good work habits that he taught me. He is one fine man, I'll tell you that. We enjoyed him then, and I still enjoy him to this day. Glen is a wonderful man.

When I was a senior at Beatrice High School, I already had enough credits to graduate and I was looking forward to it. Well, Dad worked with Reinhard Bartels, a friend whose son Don had talked him into letting me live with them when my family moved to Pawnee City so I could stay in Beatrice and graduate with my class. I really wanted to do that so I asked my dad for permission. But Dad always put work first and this time was no exception. He said, "Your old butt will be down at Pawnee City planting oats on March 1. And that was the end of that conversation. Guess where I was March 1? Pawnee City. I went only three or four weeks to the high school in Pawnee City, but that's where I graduated in 1946.

In Pawnee City, I drove a team of horses pulling a planter full of oats. The oats would drop into the ground through the funnels going down from the box. That's how it all came down the row. You had to take good care of the horses—saddle them down, then unharness them—because the horses were all you had to help get the job done.

My brothers and I often thought things would go better on the farm if our dad would just listen to us sometimes. We all took Future Farmers of America (FFA) classes in high school, and they were a great place to learn new farming methods. But my dad had no education and had learned how to farm the hard way on his parents' farm. So we'd come home from voc ag classes talking about new and better ways to do things on the farm, but Dad never would hear us out. Dad knew how to fertilize the fields only with cow, horse, and hog manure. All the farmers of his generation had learned that way. Then new ways of fertilization and new hybrids came along. Dad's mind was hard to change.

Maybe he thought about it after we were gone. Maybe he got to thinking that one of us kids was right, you know. But he never changed the way he did things.

He went on doing it the way that had worked for him all those years and was comfortable with it. See, Dad had to have things his way. He had it set up so that you had better be doing it his way, too. But by going to school, we learned some different ways to do things. A lot of times we'd tell him, "Dad you know, you ought to consider this." And he'd say, "Get your tail out to the field." He was the boss. It was that simple. His word was law.

When you grow up with your dad coming at you with sticks and razor straps when you're in trouble, that's all you know. And if you got in trouble at school, whatever happened in school was minor compared to what you were going to get when you got home. That's just the way it was. Everybody was kind of in the same boat. Dad went too far with us probably. I don't think it was all bad for us, though.

It's true that when I was growing up I thought Dad had some shortcomings, but Dad was a good Christian and a good neighbor. He told me over and over again, "Son, if you borrow something from a neighbor, you never take it back unless it's in good shape or in better shape than when you got it." So if the neighbor gave you something, any damage you did to his property you fixed before you returned it. Everybody didn't have that attitude, but that was a rule with my dad and an outstanding lesson for us.

I admired my dad. He was a very hard worker, honest, and very blunt. I've got a lot of that bluntness in me. And, of course, he expected us to do a good job at work. He would tell you that you were a good worker and kick you in the butt at the same time. He was always in the cattle business—that's all he knew. He loved farming, and he was a good farmer.

Dad and Mother both had to have a lot of strength and character to weather the Depression and us seven kids. Strangely, I think that the Depression actually made their marriage stronger for many reasons. First, where else could they go? They had a large family and everything was bleak from the money standpoint. Their difficult situation had to pull them together and make them rely on each other. Sharing common goals and valuing hard work made their relationship strong. Mother and Dad taught us honesty and integrity and expected us to live our lives based on those qualities.

Most important, Mom and Dad both had a strong Christian faith. The only time we lived in town, we went to church every Sunday. When we lived in the country, which was most of the time, we didn't always make it every Sunday because of the distance, the weather, the mud, or something else. For whatever reason, we just didn't go nearly as often. But any time that the weather was good and things were right, we were headed to church. That's the way I remember it.

Normally, we'd go to the Protestant churches. Methodist, Lutheran, or Presbyterian, whichever was the closest church to where we were living was the one we would attend on Sunday morning. Back then, people didn't go around picking out their church like folks do these days. We just went to the closest one.

I was baptized and confirmed, but I was rowdy in my younger days. That's for sure. But I always went to church, and I have always believed in God. When I went to Korea, things got pretty serious, so naturally I took my faith more seriously. I'd say that I've turned to God for help more in business as an adult than when I was a kid, though.

When my wife and I got married, we went to church all the time. We took our kids to church. We've always lived a good Christian life. See, without honesty and God, you're not going to make it anywhere. That's been the basis of our success in business—all our different businesses. And we've had quite a few of them. God's been good to us. Now I'm not saying that we didn't make some mistakes along the way, but He always guided us—sometimes around them and sometimes out of them.

2

The Happiest Home: Bill Sapp

Who we are is basic. But unless we become what God has called us to be, we are nothing. Even though my parents lost everything during the Depression and life was really tough for a long while, my mother never lost her faith. As Mother would always say, "There's a silver lining in every cloud."

I think that's one of the main reasons I had a very happy childhood. I really did. I was happier than almost anybody I knew. I never was a person who held a grudge or was hateful or anything like that. I was a happy boy.

I never felt sorry for myself. A guy doesn't feel bad without a bicycle unless all his friends have bicycles. We didn't have anything, but none of our neighbors did, either, so it really wasn't hard. We all got along and played games and had fun doing some things maybe we shouldn't have done. I was the youngest child and knew without a doubt that my mother and dad and my brothers and sisters loved me. So that was it. I was always at peace. I didn't have anything, and neither did my older brothers and sisters.

Actually, that's not true. We didn't have a lot of material possessions, but when it came to love in the family, strong values, and faith in God, we were rich.

My mother was a really gifted, wonderful, hard-working lady. And she was very positive. Mother held the dominant influence and leadership in the family and had many words of wisdom for her children, including encouragement to do well at school. A former teacher educated at Peru State College, she told us to get a good education; that was very important to her. I remember her saying many times, "Well, you boys have to get an education. We're not going to be able to help you farm or give you equipment, so you must get an education."

And she'd mention again and again that we had to get good grades. I got a report card that wasn't so good one time. And she told me, "Now you have to get good grades, Billy. You'll be proud of yourself when you do. You can do it!" Later on, both Ray and I went on to get degrees from the University of Nebraska at Lincoln (UNL). And Dean spent two and a half years at college down in Kansas.

Mother was a heck of a cook! I remember coming into the kitchen after school and smelling hot biscuits baking. I couldn't wait for them to come out of the oven! My favorite dish of hers was chicken. We raised all these chickens in our brooder house, so when we wanted chicken for dinner, we just went out and caught one. I remember eating them before they were quite big enough to eat, but we needed some meat for the table. Her fried chicken was as good as chicken gets.

There's an old saying that most Czech women can outwork their husbands. Sure enough, when I looked at my mother and aunts and uncles, that appeared to be true. Like most women of the day, Mother did all the cooking and baking. But that's not all she did.

Back in those times, the women hauled the water to put on the stove and to use for bath water. They were doing all of the sewing. They didn't have all the stuff—like refrigerators—we have now to make jobs easier. And Mom had all of us kids' diapers to wash. She did all the housework, and she raised a big garden. At night, Dad would come in, get in his rocking chair, and go to sleep. Mother, on the other hand, was still working. She made a pie or cake almost every day of her life. And then she'd sit there and quilt or crochet or knit or fix stockings. She was the first one up in the morning and probably the last one to go to bed at night.

My mother was Bohemian—full-blooded Czech, and her folks were successful farmers. Mom's mother came over from Czechoslovakia. The Czechs came over to the United States and stayed with other Czechs. The same was true for the Germans and the Swedes. Well, the country was pretty well developed when my grandmother's family came over, but neither one of my maternal grandparents could speak very good English. When I was a boy, I couldn't even talk to my grandfather because he spoke Czech all the time. In their home, they didn't speak English at all.

Naturally, my mother was fluent in Czech. My oldest two sisters could speak some Czech because Mother spoke Czech to them when they were growing up. But by the time I came around, well, the most I knew in Czech were the bits and pieces I learned from Grandpa and Grandma Hubka.

Mother's father, Joseph Hubka, originally came from Table Rock, Nebraska. Grandpa Hubka was a very hardworking man. He was also a very gifted man. He could estimate just about anything and figure out just about anything. In fact, two of his grandchildren turned out to be electrical engineers. I was in an engineering program for a while, but then I switched to teaching with math and science because I was good at that. I think that ability came from my mother's genes because on that side of the family, there were quite a few really successful children involved with higher education.

My mother's parents lived in Virginia, Nebraska, about five or six miles from Filley. We kids rode our bikes to our grandparents' house often and also got to play with our cousins while we were there.

Dad was born and raised in Illinois, near Quincy. The name Sapp is Dutch, but his mother's name was Browning, so he was probably English as well as Dutch. I didn't know my dad's dad—I don't have any recollection of him. After he died, Grandmother Sapp lived alone in Auburn, Nebraska, about forty miles away, so we hardly ever got to see her. But once in a while, we kids would all pile in the back of the family car to go visit her in Auburn.

Dad loved his children and his wife and made a lot of sacrifices for us. I know that. He was a hard worker. But Dad was limited as to what he could do because of his financing, his position, and the U.S. economy at the time. He took a business risk years before I was born and ended up going broke. He couldn't believe cattle prices would go so low, and he recognized later he should have gotten rid of the livestock sooner. But he didn't, and by the time cattle prices plummeted in 1929, there wasn't enough money to pay off the bank. Then the bank came and sold all his equipment, his farm lease, and everything else. My older sisters remember the good times when Dad was successful before the Crash. He had, at one time, a very successful farmstead and a lot of cattle.

I don't want to paint a bad picture of my father, though. He was not a bad man at all. My father was limited in his education and in his business experience, however. In fact, he had no business experience. The only experience he really had was farming with his parents. And he learned how they thought farming should be done and that's how he farmed as an adult himself. I think in all fairness, considering how he was raised, he did the best he could.

I know his ways, or lack of them, were hard sometimes on my mom, though. For example, Dad wasn't the best, in my opinion, at keeping financial records. So Mother kept the records. She was always on him to do a better job of that because they didn't have much money to start with. I remember a lot of times he would write checks with no deposits being made, and then they'd be overdrawn at the bank.

Dad made all the decisions about farming, but I'm not sure how well his other decisions stuck, especially those affecting the children, considering Mother's influence on the workings of the family. There is a story about Brother Dean's name that proves the point. Mother had apparently named all three girls and the two older boys, as well. So, when she was expecting again, she asked Dad if he would like to name the baby. Dad had a good friend along the way named Harold, so Dad told Mother that he would like to name their baby boy Harold. So they did. But apparently, before Mother had told Dad he could pick out the baby's name, she already had chosen the name Dean. And so Dean's full name is Harold Dean Sapp.

Now what came next may show a bit of my mother's dominance. Instead of calling the baby Harold, as was the plan, the moment they got home, she started calling him Dolly Dean. Even I knew him a little bit as Dolly Dean. Growing up, I never called him anything other than Dean. After many years went by, I found out when he went to sign his name to something that his name was really Harold! The only time that boy was called Harold was on the day he was born.

Now my given name is really William, and I have the only name out of all of us brothers that has a given nickname to go with it. When I was in grade school, they always called me Billy, but I graduated from high school as Bill. And I had no problems with that. It could even have been Willy or Will, or William. But I was always called either Bill or Billy, so Bill Sapp is my name basically. I didn't have to change it. I was in the clear!

In his own way, Dad did a lot of good things for us that I just took for granted. I think all the rest of the children did, too; I wasn't the only one. We just don't talk much about the support that he gave us. And I am grateful for all he did. We always talk about everything that Mother did for us, but we don't even touch the subject of our dad supporting us. He loved my mother and did what he could to help his children.

The first home I remember living in—a very old house that needed a lot of repair—was in Filley. It was really cold in that house, but our church was just a little ways up the block. The next house we moved to was the Weston Farm. It was an older house by the railroad tracks, but we could at least have a cow there. We needed a cow for milk. In fact, I remember that it was an old Jersey cow. She would give us her milk and cream, and every dairy product our whole family ate came from that one cow.

After that, we lived in a little brown house farther out— Sorenson House—named after the original owner of the farm. And then we moved on to Beatrice. After that, Pawnee City. Then to Lewiston and then to Diller. As you can see, we moved around a lot, but I never much minded it.

Because we went to a consolidated school, even if we moved to another house, we'd still go to the same school. When we did move to other school districts like Beatrice, we didn't have any trouble making new friends. My brothers and I were friendly people, so it didn't seem like a big thing for us to make new friends. In fact, in a short time, we had a lot of friends and knew a lot of people and neighbors, too, because we were playing sports.

But I think the moving around was really hard on our parents. It was a heck of a lot tougher on them than on us because they had so many things to do. Over and over again Mother and Dad had to meet new neighbors, start going to a new church, and try to fix up another house. Whenever we moved into another house, we did a lot of wallpaper-ing—my mother was a good wallpaperer. We did a lot of painting, too. She and Dad always fixed things up to the best of their ability to make everything look a little nicer.

Before the good times started again in the '40s, there were the hard times. We learned early that waxed cartons work better than newspapers to plug up shoes with holes in them. There was tar paper on our front door. People on the WPA, like Mother and Dad, got only $45 a month on that program. Mom and Dad paid $5 each month for the farmhouse, $5 for our old car, $5 or $6 to Sears, and $5 or $6 to Montgomery Ward.

Mother had about $20 to buy groceries for seven kids. Sometimes we had bean soup with a little bone in it, and she always made Jell-O for dessert. My brothers and I also went hunting and trapping. We killed a lot of rabbits and went home and cleaned them. Then we'd have jackoburgers. That was when we took rabbit and hamburger and mixed them together to make the meat go further.

Even during those hard times of the Depression, people cared about each other and were still very good-natured. Because many people were suffering economic hardship, acts of kindness meant a lot.

One of my earliest memories is of a kind railroad conductor throwing us a newspaper—a *Beatrice Times* or *Beatrice Daily Sun*—every day as the train chugged right by our farmhouse. We lived out of town a few miles, so the only paper we had was that one he gave us. We didn't pay for the paper; we had no money. It was just a little thing, but it was nice of him and the railroad to do that.

We had no electricity. Most of the neighbors didn't have electricity, either. We had only kerosene or gas lamps. Fortunately, in the mid-'40s, The Rural Electrical Association (REA), funded by a federal program, brought electricity to our part of the state. In the last farmhouse we lived in, when

I was a senior in high school, the folks bought a refrigerator. I remember we got ice cream right away and got some other stuff because we had a better way of keeping the food cold.

Mom made all the girls' clothes from scratch. In those days, the feed companies would make printed cloth bags. Then the people that had chickens would use that cloth for all kinds of things. Well, we had some chickens back then, and Mother would take those feedbags and make curtains, or even dresses for the girls or herself, out of that print cloth. It was actually pretty common back then to make clothes out of those sacks.

We didn't have much in the way of clothes. I just had a little pair of pants and a little T-shirt and nothing much else. It didn't take very many clothes for us brothers—just a pair of pants and a little pair of shorts, and that was it.

When we were very small, we would get a pair of shoes in the fall. When they wore out, usually by the spring, then we just wouldn't have any shoes. No shoes. We had no stockings, either. We were just barefoot. You washed your feet before you went to bed at night. And then when our feet grew a little, Mother ordered new shoes in the fall from Sears or Montgomery Ward.

Because we went around barefoot so much during the summer months, we sometimes got thorns or nails stuck in our feet, but they'd heal. In fact, my mother was very good at doctoring. It was a good thing, because we had no insurance in those days, and we just didn't have any money to pay doctor bills.

Mother made her own remedies. Those remedies actually did work, too. If you had a stomachache, you took baking soda. If you were coming down with a cold, she'd give you another remedy, and put you to bed. An enema for a fever. If you got cut or anything like that, she'd put kerosene from our kerosene lamps on it. Or grease to kill the germs.

We didn't have any money to pay a dentist, so nobody went. In fact, I didn't see one until I went to the Army. As I recall, I saw a doctor only once during my childhood. That was after I jumped into a pond, split my foot open, and went to the doctor to have it sewn up. See, we had this dog named Rex that we would go hunting with. And we'd go swimming in the pond with Rex, too. That dog would pull us across the pond like you wouldn't believe. Well, one day, we went down to the pond we swam in during the summertime. We liked to run and dive into it. This time when I came out after swimming a bit, my foot was all bloody. I didn't even know what had happened. I guess my foot caught on an old piece of barbed wire when I dived into the pond, and the barbed wire slit the top of my foot open. I was bleeding like a stuck hog, so they took me home.

Dad and Mom took me into Filley, and we went to the doctor there. Mom and Dad had to hold me down because the doctor didn't give me anything to numb the pain. He just used a needle, kind of like a big horseshoe needle, and some thread. It didn't hurt much going down through, but it hurt a little bit when he came up from the other side. Maybe it hurt more than a little bit. I yelled and I hollered, but they held me. Then when he was through with each stitch, the string was left there. He pulled it together and tied a knot in it. And then he went on to the next one, and he pulled the string together and tied a knot in that one, too. After he did that several times, he put the antiseptic on. After that, I went home. I still have a big scar from my first visit to the doctor. It wasn't too bad, though. I tell you, we were always doing something exciting.

We had one sister, Zelma, who didn't get sick—ever. You know, the rest of us got the mumps and measles and whatever else came along. But she never got any of those diseases! When she got married and had her own children, her kids had a lot of different sicknesses, but she never got any of them, either. To this day, I think a good cold is the only sickness Zelma has had in her entire life.

She must have some kind of a natural immunity, because in those days, everybody drank out of the same dipper in a water pail in the kitchen. We went to the well, got a bucket of water, put it out there in the kitchen, and that's what you drank out of. If you needed water for anything else, that's where you'd get it.

During the wintertime, all of us would try to keep warm in the living room by staying near the big stove stoked with coal and wood and cobs. At night, Mother would heat up those heavy irons that she used to iron clothes with on the stove. She'd wrap them in some old towels she had, and then we'd take them upstairs and put them at the bottom of the bed to keep our feet warm. The feather beds would help, too, but we'd still get up in the morning with snow in the house because the windows were cracked. The bedrooms were cold and I mean *cold*.

Some of the houses we lived in probably shouldn't have been still standing. I think the folks paid about five dollars a month rent for the whole house. The landlord wouldn't do much; on sixty dollars a year, how much maintenance could he do?

I remember that the school board for the country school didn't have enough money to even buy a bat and ball for our school, so each student brought a dime, and the teacher bought a bat and a ball. Some kids were playing the game Keep Away with a boy named Pud one day. He wanted that ball so bad, but they weren't going to give it to him. The more they weren't giving it to him, the harder the kid played. When he finally got the ball, he said, "I want to tell you people, I got a dime in this ball, and if you keep playing Keep Away with me, I'm going to cut my dime's worth right out of the middle. Well, funny how everybody decided they wouldn't play Keep Away any more with Pud because he might ruin their ball! And they did not want that!

We all played with the neighbor boys—it seemed there were a lot more neighbors in those days. One family lived next to us and then another lived just down the road. Then there'd be another family across the road. If they had any kids, they would come over and we'd play together.

Since there wasn't much chance to get away from the farm, we made our own fun right there. But sometimes there was a fine line between fun and trouble. One day, Lee, Dean, our two cousins on our mother's side—Elmer and Laurie Hubka—and I came up with a plan that sounded like a lot of fun. We would ride our bicycles down to a bridge a quarter or a half mile from the track and sit around under it smoking "cigarettes." The "cigarettes" my cousin Elmer brought were really just weeds from the meadow rolled up like cigarettes, but we pretended they were the real thing.

Now the oldest boys are the ones who make the decisions in a group like that, not the littlest kids. Laurie and I were the youngest ones there. We were really young, understand—no more than third or fourth grade. We were just along for the ride really. I remember that I wanted to be with the older boys that day, though. And the older boys decided to make a bonfire there because we had only a couple of matches among us all.

So they made a little fire, and it was going pretty good. They'd light these cigarettes, and sometimes they were all smoking the same cigarette because, you know, they didn't have that many of them. To keep the fire from going out, they kept putting more and more stuff on it. It really got going good. Now this bonfire was burning in a slough, which was a low spot where a lot of grass and stuff grew. And then there was a neighbor's wheat field next to the site of our fire. It was the time of year that the grass was getting dry because there hadn't been much rain.

When the fire started to spread to the field, we had to take off our little pants and beat the fire out! Then we thought, "Now what are we going to do?" We couldn't go home with our clothes full of ashes and everything else. We sure weren't going to tell them we were smoking or we'd definitely get a whipping when Dad got home. We didn't want that.

So we dreamed up a story. Well, we had to say something. We all agreed we wouldn't tell what really happened. The older boys, Lee and Dean, told Mother and Dad that some sparks from the train must have caused that fire, but we put it out. We were heroes!

Yeah, the train did it. And there was no spanking. I think that later on the older boys might have told the truth, though. I'm sure Mom and Dad found out somehow that we weren't heroes after all. But when you're the littlest kid standing with a bunch of older boys, what are you supposed to do?

For fun that didn't get us into trouble, we played all kinds of games. We played pinochle. We played pitch. We played checkers. We played Chinese checkers. Outside we played hide-and-go-seek and pickup sticks. At night after we got everything done, especially in the winter, we would sit around the table and play card games before we went to bed. And we were all competitive, so we had lots of fun.

We'd keep score on long card games. I remember my mother would say, "Now, Billy, bid your hand, bid your hand." She would encourage me when we played pitch because I was the youngest and was always afraid to bid. Then she'd urge me to bid a little more. I learned that if you actually made a bid, it wasn't so bad. It was more important that I tried rather than just sat there and did nothing.

My folks would go to all the neighbors' houses and do the same thing. During those years, nobody had much, so you'd go wherever there was a game. They'd have popcorn and cold water from the well, and that was it. They always had popcorn because everybody had popcorn. But popcorn and cold water was really a treat. In fact, I still love popcorn. And so did everyone in the family.

My brothers and I were competitive with one another growing up, but we would band together if anybody else would mess with one of us. If you had trouble with one, you'd probably have trouble with us all, so most people wouldn't pull anything. Lee was probably the best fighter out of all of the brothers. Lee was very good, and he was kind of aggressive in his fighting—more so than anybody else was, anyway.

Dad got us boxing gloves one year. Lee took on Dean, and then Dean took on me. Dean was older, but very small, so we were about the same size. Years later, Dean would tell me, "You almost had me whipped several times, so I'd try to sock you in the nose. Pretty soon, I'd get a good punch at it, and then your nose would start to bleed. Then we'd have to quit because there'd be blood all over everything." So that's how he did it!

We boxed outside—in the yard, mostly. Or sometimes in the barn if the barn was open in the summer. Sometimes Dad was there so one of us wouldn't get hurt; most of the time that was when we had the gloves on. But when we didn't have the gloves on, we'd fight anywhere! Outside, in the kitchen. Anywhere.

Even though we moved around a lot, I played sports, and so did all my brothers.

We were not great stars, but we always played on the high school teams. And we were above average. The good thing when you go to such a small school is that you always get to play and watch your brothers play.

Basketball was my favorite sport, and we played a lot of it out on the farm. Because finances were tight, we used the steel band that used to go around barrels to build our own basketball hoop. The hoop was fastened with bolts, and we played just around in kind of a circle. We had an old basketball that Dad got us. Dad helped us, you know. Ray and I always played against Lee and Dean. We played when we'd get everything done; we'd play until we couldn't see anymore. It was totally dark, and you could hardly see the ball. We'd play and play and play basketball out there.

Discipline was a very big part of my growing up. And Dad was a force to be reckoned with. He was probably raised with a lot of discipline himself. And I think both of our parents felt that in any kind of family, especially one with young boys, the father needed to keep them in line if they did something wrong. These psychology books say that you shouldn't spank a child or discipline a child, but I never felt—and I don't think any of my brothers ever felt—that when Dad gave us a spanking it was wrong. I just figured that if you did something wrong, you should be punished. And when you got punished, that was just part of the knocks of life.

I remember one time when we lived on the Weston Farm. My brothers and I were fighting quite a little bit around that time. Dad was working for the WPA then and he told Mother one morning before he left for work, "If those boys get to fighting today, you let me know." And he told all of us boys out there, "I'm telling you boys, there's no fighting today, and if you fight, you're going to get a spanking." So we said, "Yes, Dad, yes, Dad."

Well, the day went on and we were out doing something, Dean and me. One thing led to another and we ended up having a disagreement of sorts. We really went at it. We didn't just get a little mad; we went at it tooth and nail with our little fists swinging, grabbing each other, throwing each other to the ground, and rolling over and over. We didn't keep track of the time. In fact, we weren't even thinking about the time.

When Dad pulled up into the driveway with his old car, we looked up and suddenly remembered what he had told us that morning. Dad jumped out of the car. And Dean took off at a dead run. And I took after him. Being the younger of us two brothers, I wasn't quite as fast as Dean, so Dad caught up with me first, but he went right past because he wanted to get Dean—the older one. I headed for the house to get Mother's protection but got a spanking later anyway.

Now if Mother wasn't happy with you, she would talk to you and let you know. Mother would tell you what was wrong, and she'd explain it to you: "Now, Bill, you should do this. You have a sense of responsibility, and if you're going to be a good citizen, you know, you've got to do this."

I think all of us respected our mother very highly. If Mother had an opinion, and Dad had a different one, we would end up feeling that Mother was probably right.

But our parents were not the only disciplinarians in our home. Out of all of the sisters, Veloura was the one with the most authority. When you did something bad, you had to turn around and go sit in the corner. There were several times that we had to put on dunce hats, but I don't think it was very often. I do know sometimes we had four corners full of boys and sometimes one or two corners occupied, depending on what we had done wrong. When all of us boys were sitting in the corners at the same time, usually it meant we'd been disagreeing about something and had gotten into a little fistfight. And the girls would break us up, telling us we shouldn't be fighting all the time.

If you did something really upsetting, you'd sit there longer than if you just did a little thing. You'd have to sit there, let's say fifteen minutes, hypothetically. After you'd sat there maybe ten minutes, you'd say, "Oh, it's time to get up and go."

"No, no, no, you got five more minutes," Veloura would say.

"It's time to go," you'd say.

"No, no, no, you got two more minutes," she'd say.

Veloura knew what she was talking about because they had a clock in the house. And so you'd sit there. But if somebody didn't do what Veloura told him to or said, "You can't make me," or "I'm going to leave," he would get a spanking from our dad with the razor strap when our parents got home. So we did not upset that system because we didn't want to get a spanking. And it was a good system. It was a really good system.

And then there was Zelma. The only teacher that really stood out to me was my sister Zelma. She taught me my entire eighth grade year at a rural school called Hillsdale. Zelma was a very good teacher, but she was also good at making me feel guilty. That part of the story will come a little later. Anyway, each week she would give me either a quarter or fifty cents for lighting the heat stove at school every day. I always liked school and was good at it, especially in math and history, and I was happy to have the job.

Because it was a country school, there was just an iron stove and it was my job to take care of it. I'd put the cobs in the stove, put a little kerosene on them, and then light a match. When the cobs got going, I'd put some coal on top of the cobs so we'd have a good fire. I'd known how to make fire for the stove ever since I could remember. If you want to get warm, you get the fire going. When it was time, I took the ashes out of the stove and put them on the path going to the outhouses and the cob house.

One Friday while Zelma was my teacher during the spring of '45, we had some trouble on the way home from school. Our family had an old Dodge, and although we walked the gravel road the one mile to school most of the time, this day Zelma got to take the family car.

Well, when school got out that day, a couple of other boys and I went outside to play a little ball. Pretty soon Zelma came to the door and said, "Billy, get the stove taken care of." Now I don't know if Zelma was in such a hurry because her beau, Kenny, was back from the Navy, and they were going out or what, but she sure was rushing that day. I didn't want to go home yet, so I was messing around a little. Then Zelma told me again, "You're supposed to go in and take care of your stove, do you understand?" And I said, "Oh, yes, yes, yes!" So, I dropped my ball, ran in, and hurried up and got the ashes out.

By this time, Zelma had gotten everything she wanted into the car. As we got into the car, she was still saying things like, "You know, you have a responsibility…" and on and on about an eighth-grade boy's duty when his older sister teaches.

Well, back in those days you had the gear shifts in the middle of the floor. When Zelma started the car and put it in reverse to back out of the drive, she was still quite busy lecturing me about something or other, and she backed right into the flagpole! The flagpole fell over and it bent the rear bumper on Dad's car. We got out and looked, and then Zelma just broke down and cried. She just bawled. And then she started blaming me for the whole thing. She told me it never would have happened if I would've done what I was supposed to do. I was the scapegoat as far as I was concerned. But I couldn't do anything. You know, I couldn't drive or anything, so I didn't say a word. You know when you're wrong and someone's mad at you, what can you do? You're just better off to keep quiet and take it.

So we drove home. And I didn't think much about it, but, of course, she had to explain everything to Dad—how she bent that rear bumper. And then she had to call the school board, and they had to get that flagpole fixed. Zelma was worried about her job, but I don't think it was that bad. The school board probably just grinned and then fixed it, but I don't know. I was just an eighth grader, and what does an eighth grader know about what's going on in the world?

Dad came in then and said to me, "Well, you weren't doing what you were supposed to be doing at the school. That was irresponsible, and you know it." So he gave me a light spanking. You know, he hit me but not real hard. Wham, and that was it.

I never felt bad about it, though. I always thought, "Well, there were a lot of spankings that I should have gotten that I didn't get." But this was the only one that I can ever remember where I felt I was unjustly spanked. But I had no grudge towards my sister or my dad or anybody. I just thought, well, you know, I got caught one time when I wasn't guilty, but that's okay.

As far as the chores went in general, I never really thought about it at the time, but looking back, being the youngest might have been more of an advantage than a disadvantage. Ray had to go work for our neighbors, and whatever he earned, he had to come home and give half of it to Dad and Mom to help out.

When we moved up to Beatrice, I was just a seventh grader. Back then, I was expected to gather the eggs, which is kind of a mediocre task. My other task was to put the cobs behind the kitchen stove because that is where we stored the cobs. We always put cobs in the stove to get the stove warmed up in the morning when we'd first come out. Everybody had a task, and that was mine.

Right around that same time, for some reason I became very anxious to milk a cow. We had some milk cows there, and Mom and Dad finally let me do the big job—milking the cow. Well, I milked her a few times, and pretty soon that was my chore. In fact, soon I had to milk two cows. And pretty soon, I wasn't so anxious to milk the cows even though I probably had the least number of anyone to milk back then. The older brothers had more even though they had other chores as well. And pretty soon I was driving a tractor, too.

But then we moved to the Pawnee farm when I was thirteen, I believe. My mother would come down and milk two cows to my one and get more milk from each of them. She would come down and help me because my brothers didn't come in from the field until dark. Since we milked twice a day, it was several hours of milking.

I remember I got so tired of milking cows that one day I said, "Lord, when I grow up, please don't make me a dairy farmer because I don't want to milk the cows!" I didn't want my future life to include milking a bunch of cows. I just didn't want to do it.

Sometimes there'd be a tussle about farming with us boys on one side—how we thought a certain task should be done—and Dad on the other. There'd be some discussions and a few arguments. Occasionally, we brothers won the argument, but most of the time, we did it Dad's way. Some techniques we modified and did them our way, whether he knew it or not.

As the years went by, though, Dad seemed to listen to us more and more, and it seemed like the times were starting to change. He actually accepted some of the ideas that we suggested. Dad saw his neighbors and friends had started doing things differently and his old-fashioned ways seemed very time-consuming—even to him.

He did make some changes then. For example, the old 10-20 tractor and John Deere Model B had their lugs converted to rubber tires and tubes. After that change, we got better efficiency, traction, and ride. We found out later in life that some of the actions that he wanted to take were absolutely those we suggested to him in the first place! I guess that's typical of young boys and their dad.

Our mother was the prayer warrior of the family. She was the person in our family who was most committed to the Lord. She was the one who talked about God. She was the one who led us down a spiritual path. Mom would say that this is wrong, or say, "God's watching you whether I'm watching or not." She'd talk a lot about Jesus and God with all her children. She took us to Sunday school and then Bible school in the summertime when we were little children. My favorite Bible story growing up was about David and Goliath and Joseph—you know, his Coat of Many Colors. As we grew up, Mother encouraged us to go to church every Sunday, but we didn't always go.

I really can't even remember my dad ever really talking about Jesus Christ, except to use His name in vain. But I never thought that was bad growing up. I just noticed that he had a bad habit, you know. If a cow was kicking or something like that, I learned it was okay for me to swear because men do that. Not only did my dad do it, but also sometimes my neighbor or someone else I was working for did. In fact, the truth of it is, there were very few men in my life while I was growing up who didn't swear.

In Diller, Nebraska, around 1948, I was a high school student, and I had been getting a little wild around the edges. You know, I was running with a certain crowd. When we went to dances when I was a teenager, we'd go down to Kansas and drink 3.2 beer. There were several dance halls, and we'd dance with the girls and then come home. The folks didn't really say too much about it. It was kind of like drinking with the boys was okay.

Well, right around my beer-drinking time, I met a man by the name of Keith Hayes. Keith was the head of the Methodist Youth Fellowship—the MYF—at the Methodist church there in town. Keith Hayes showed me that I was at a point in my life where I either needed to accept Christ or not. He put it very directly. "If you accept Him, then you get to go to heaven. And if you don't accept Him, you'll go to hell," he told me.

Well, I read all the books of the Bible that year. I think it was because of Keith's influence in my life that I accepted Jesus as my Lord and Savior at a later time. Jesus is the way. That seed got planted.

When I was a sophomore at Fairbury Junior College, I played on the football team. I had several jobs, too, but never seemed to have much to show for them. I didn't get to socialize too much because of my lack of funds, but for a special occasion every month or so, my friends and I would go to a dance hall with our girlfriends.

One night a friend of mine, Noel Folkers, called me and asked me if I wanted to go to a dance in Wilber with him and his girl. And I said, "Well, I guess so" and I told him I'd call Donna, the girl I'd been dating for a while. She said she'd like to go, so Noel picked us up with his girlfriend, and we were on our way to Wilber, Nebraska. We ended up leaving my old '37 Ford in Diller that night.

On the way, we stopped in a little town called Harbin. There was a tavern and a grain elevator there, and that's all there was. Well, we stopped in at that tavern and wanted to buy a case of beer. I was eighteen, and Noel, I think, was eighteen, so we were both minors. Back then, a number of places would sell alcohol to minors, but you kind of had to pick the right time. You wanted to go in there and see that there weren't a lot of other people in the place because if there were, the owner probably wouldn't sell to you because he could get in trouble. Anyway, that night the man sold us a case of beer.

So we drove up to Wilber, Nebraska, and went into the dance. And while we were there, we met some of our old friends from Odell who also were going to Fairbury Junior College. They asked us, "Do you have a beer?" And we answered, "Yeah, we got a case out in the car."

So we told our girls that we were going to go out in the car and have a beer with these guys. And we went out to the car and started drinking and talking. I was sitting on the passenger's side, Noel was sitting in the driver's seat, and the two boys from Odell were in the back.

All of a sudden, my door flew open and two policemen were standing there. They grabbed me and my beer right out of the car. I asked them, "What's wrong?" One of the officers barked, "It's illegal to drink beer on the streets of Wilber."

They told me they were going to haul me down to the police station. Now there were three other boys in the car, too, but I guess the policemen felt that they weren't big enough or strong enough to take all four of us. The policemen put the beer in their pocket then, and started literally dragging me down the street.

I did not want to go.

My first thought was, "Oh, my!" Here if I was going to jail, that would be the end of my college. And I did want to go to college. If I couldn't go to college, then that would be the end of my playing on the football team. So going to jail would be the end of everything that I really wanted to do. And then when I got down there to the station, I would have to explain to them where we got the beer because if you were under twenty-one, then you were a minor, and you weren't supposed to have beer. So what was I going to do? Well, I decided, and this was not necessarily an intelligent decision, that I was not going to go.

Since I was playing football and was quite strong, I pushed away the one policeman and then hit him with my elbow as hard as I could. And then I pulled the other officer around in front of me and hit him with my fist. Then I broke loose, and I took off on a dead run. Well, my friends saw all this from the car, so they drove around the block and picked me up.

We stayed off the streets for a while, and then had the boys pick up our girls. We took the back roads all the way home. We thought the sheriff and the state patrol and everybody was after us, but I'm sure they weren't. At that time, though, I didn't think that was the end of it. We finally made it back home to Diller and got my little car. Then I drove it home and got into bed.

And I really tossed and turned that night. I got to thinking about what I learned in MYF. One of the things was that we were either going to go to heaven or to hell. And I thought to myself, "You know, those guys could have shot you." And if I died at that time, I was pretty sure I'd go to the devil. So I said, "Dear Lord, dear Jesus, if you're real (and Jesus is real by the way), I want you to come into my life. I'm not doing too good. I'm kind of striking out. And you're my Lord and…."

Then I fell off to sleep.

The police never came back after me. They didn't know who I was. No bells, no whistles. But my entire life was changed. I do drink a little wine at our church every now and again, but that was the last beer I had. I think that night was a blessing because it was then I decided that I was going to go to hell if I kept doing what I was doing. And I didn't want to go to hell; I wanted to go to heaven. But, if I was going to get to heaven, then I had to accept Jesus. So I did accept Him, all right—that night.

And it did change my whole life. I didn't smoke or drink beer my whole life after that experience. I never really smoked anyway except as a kid on a trial basis. All of that was taboo from that moment forward, and I went the other way. I chose to go the other way. But really, that instant had more to do with my life than anything else. It was a huge turning point. My whole life, at all the family gatherings, always at Christmas, and each and every day, I have always said thanks before I eat. If you eat with me today, you will hear me give thanks for my food. I'm a committed Christian.

Part II

Going Our Separate Ways

Peace I leave with you, my peace I give unto you:
not as the world giveth, give I unto you.
Let not your heart be troubled, neither let it be afraid.
—John 14:27

3

Moving On: Lee Sapp

I remember an old picture of the four of us brothers when we all were in the service. Ray and I both have our Navy uniforms on. We were both pharmacists' mates—corpsmen, they called us. Bill was in his Army uniform, and Dean was in his Air Force uniform. All four of us boys joined the military, see. I think that picture showed our parents were proud that all their boys served their country.

The day that Pearl Harbor was bombed on December 7, 1941, was no big deal to us kids. I'm sure Mom and Dad understood the full effects of it better than we did, but I don't think anyone realized in any way, shape, or form how big an event it was when it happened. As we kids got older, we'd see newspapers, and we'd see books about Pearl Harbor. Then we learned the real facts, but we didn't realize them before then. Actually, Ray may have understood better than the rest of us did. He was the oldest brother and served in World War II.

After graduating from Pawnee City High School in 1946, I didn't stick around long. I moved back to Beatrice when I was seventeen and worked at Paul Henderson's filling station. I stayed with my oldest sister, Irene, and her husband, Guy; in fact, I lived with them until I went into the service.

I can't honestly say that I was thinking much about what I was going to do with my life at that time. When you're that age, you don't think about those things the way you do later on. I was fixin' to go into the service; I knew that. I'd had no real work experience off the farm at that point and certainly no business experience back then. Paul Henderson owned a Ford dealership that had a filling station in front. So I worked full-time—eight hours a day—at that filling station for about twelve months.

During my spare time, I socialized with Guy and Irene quite a lot. And, I still had some friends that I had played basketball with in high school. Then there were a couple of girls that I had dated back in high school, but I didn't really date much then. Mostly, I just worked.

Upstairs from the filling station I worked at was a VFW Club. It was 1948 and the trouble in Korea was heating up. One night I went up to the VFW for a drink after work, and a petty officer was signing guys up like crazy. That's when I decided it was time for me to join the Navy. I'd wanted to join the service for a while, so I volunteered.

When I first joined the Navy, I went to boot camp and then the Navy put me through pharmacy school. Now when I say "pharmacy," I'm talking about everything from handling bedpans to filling prescriptions. I learned all about bandaging, setting legs, giving shots, and other minor stuff. See, we didn't have enough medical training to do what doctors could.

As soon as I graduated, I was transferred to San Diego Naval Hospital. A commander there, Commander Angel, thought the world of me and actually wanted me to become a doctor. He even offered to work a deal where the government would pay for me to go all through school for it. But I said, "No, I'm going to Korea!" That tells you how smart I as. Well, you know, you got to be young and dumb sometime. I ran into a lot of nice officers and enlisted people, but I really looked up to that doctor.

You know how love is. The minute I laid eyes on Helene, I thought she was beautiful, but it wasn't until a couple of months later that I knew I was in love with her. My blue-eyed future wife was a Navy nurse at the San Diego Naval Hospital. Helene was a dedicated nurse and worked in tuberculosis surgery until she herself got tuberculosis. She was the hardest-working nurse there was—well organized, meticulous, and stubborn. I'm telling you, she was good. I loved the way she talked and had so much integrity. And she was pretty, too!

She was my boss. Now, I didn't report directly to her, but she was the head nurse on the same ward where I worked. She was up two or three levels from me and had nurses under her. She called the shots on the ward, and what she said would filter down to us corpsmen. If I was on the ward, she was my boss.

Eventually, though, Helene and I got to date, and we fell in love during the year we worked together at the San Diego Naval Hospital. But then they put me in charge of the post office at San Diego Hospital. The captain on the base there and I got along beautifully. He was very nice to me.

One day he told me that he had a lady friend, and, of course, his wife, who lived on the base with him, didn't know about her. He said, "Sapp, just don't deliver any of my girlfriend's letters to my home." He let me know that I had better not rat him out or they would be "pipin' air" to keep me alive. That's an old Navy expression that means you're not seeing any daylight because you're in jail.

The job running the post office was a good one. I could go into the commissary at any time and the Navy furnished me with a car to get around in and deliver mail to the captain and vice captain's places. I also got to deliver the mail to the nurses' quarters where Helene stayed.

After I worked at the post office for about eight or nine months, I decided that I'd really like to go off with the Marine Corps for a while. See, the Marine Corps has no medical bureau, so the Navy furnishes all the medical people for the Marine Corps. Always has, probably always will.

I told my captain that I wanted to go over to the Marine Corps. I was already a pharmacist, or corpsman, see. And he said, "You're crazy. You're just a kid. Why does anybody want to go to war and get killed? You don't want to go over there to Korea. They're killing people!"

And then I went home to visit my parents. They were sitting there, worried. Then my dad took me over to U.S. Senator Wherry's house, where I told the senator the truth about wanting to go with the Marine Corps. And he told me, basically, that I was not being very smart. It was pretty much the same story, you know. And he was right. But, when you're young and full of it, you don't always see that.

Sixty days later, I was at Camp Pendleton, a Marine Corps base in California. We called that base "Poopin' 'n' Snoopin'." You know, you'd crawl around on your belly with a rifle and do a lot of hard things. Ninety days later, I was in Seoul, Korea. I had transferred to the Marines and started wearing a Marine uniform, but was still actually a Navy man and a pharmacist.

Korea is where I really grew up and became a man. I left for Korea at the end of 1950. When I got to Seoul, they gave me a map and told me that my outfit was about twenty-five miles in a certain direction. They had a good map for me and the other corpsmen and Marines to follow, but the roads wound into the hills and over small mountains, and dead people were lying around everywhere. I had already seen dead people because I had the morgue watch in San Diego. On morgue watch, I had to stay there all night and make sure that nobody bothered the dead bodies. No one could have messed with them because the building was locked down, but they always made sure a corpsman was there anyway.

Now the Marines had some choice words for us corpsmen. Because we were in a different branch of the service, they treated us like dogs—until they got hit or sick or were going on liberty. Then, they loved us!

I found that my military training, at both boot camp and Camp Pendleton, came in very handy later on down the line. It built toughness in you. I used to think that the skills they taught were completely unnecessary—useless in the real world. They were things I never thought of when I was home on the farm by myself. But I was young and stupid. I hadn't been in combat yet.

One night in Korea, I was one of forty people up on a hill that was surrounded by the Chinese. Our commander, General Chester Pulley, was a Marine. I was a nobody then and should not have been up there. The only reason that I was there was that I was the medical guy associated with General Pulley and several of the other officers going up there that night.

Somehow, the enemy found out the general's whereabouts, and they surrounded the hill. Although the hill was surrounded by the enemy, General Pulley and the Air Force somehow managed to wipe out a bunch of them. Then the Chinese just took off running.

I heard shots that night, but I never got hurt or even scratched. I think only two people got hurt in that whole deal. I saw some action but nothing serious. It was on that hill that I realized that all of that training was very important.

In January 1952, I returned from Korea and was stationed at Chicago Naval Base. And there I was, back in Navy clothes again. As new soldiers graduated from boot camp, they were put on trains going every direction to their assignments. Every train had to have a corpsman on it in case someone got sick, and I was one of those corpsmen riding the rails. And that was to be the last job I'd have in the Navy.

Although our military experiences were in some ways different and in some ways the same, all four of us Sapp brothers learned lessons we would never forget. Lessons about preparedness, hard work, skill, trust, loyalty, and faith. These lessons, as well as those learned on the farm, helped lay the foundation for our professional and personal lives when we returned home.

4

Beyond Nebraska: Bill Sapp

All of us boys were raised to love God and country, so when we got old enough to join the military, we all were eager to serve.

Dad was as patriotic as anyone, but when it came to his youngest son going into the military, he didn't like that idea at all. He already had three sons serving, so he could've gotten me deferred, but I refused to let my dad take that step. I told him that all of my brothers went, so I was going, too. I knew he really needed help on the farm, but I wasn't going to be denied the chance to serve my country.

I didn't join the service right out of high school, though. Mother had encouraged all of us boys to go to college and thought it was really important that we receive an education. She pounded it into us that it was something we should do. So, I attended Fairbury Junior College, working my way through school with a couple of part-time jobs and playing guard on the football team.

After I graduated in 1951 with an associate degree in education, I took my two-year teaching certificate and taught seventh and eighth grades in Polk, Nebraska. I was also the assistant coach for the high school football coach, Art Phillips, a very nice guy. At nineteen, I wasn't much older than the players. In fact, some of the seniors were probably as old as I was. As assistant coach, I wasn't the leader of the pack, but I loved the job.

I've been asked what the best part of my first year of teaching was, and I'd have to say it was meeting Lucille, the young woman who would become my wife. She was a complete joy and just swept me off my feet. Lucille had taught kindergarten and first grade for a year before I arrived at the school.

Around Christmastime, the teachers drew names to exchange gifts. I was given Lucille's name. Later on, I found out there was a plot. No drawing was actually involved in my case. Anyway, I found a little sterling silver chain bracelet with a little key and a heart and gave it to her for a Christmas present. That may have seemed a little strange, considering we hadn't even started dating yet. We did start going out after that, and by spring I'd asked her if she'd marry me. Thank goodness, she said she would. By the way, she's still got that little silver bracelet.

My dad needed my help on the farm the summer of that year, so, at age twenty, I went back home. At that point, Lucille and I were engaged to be married, so she came down and stayed with another teacher in Beatrice, Nebraska, to be closer to me in Diller. That was the only reason she moved there. Lucille got a summer job there in Beatrice, thank goodness. I was thinking that she would stay back home in Chappell, Nebraska, that summer because her family lived there. I figured I would never get to see her because Chappell, out west in the panhandle, is a long, long way from Diller, which is located in the southeast corner of the state. But Lucille staying in Beatrice meant that she was only fourteen or fifteen miles away. Dad and I would work long, hard hours all day long and then late into the evening. If it rained or something, I'd get to go to Beatrice to see Lucille; otherwise, I'd have to wait until the weekends.

That summer of '52, I was on my way to being drafted. As I mentioned, my father did not want me to go. I was the last of four brothers, and the three before me were already in the service.

A couple years prior, Ray, who had fought in World War II, was in the Reserves back home and Uncle Sam had been paying for his tuition at the University of Nebraska. But then the Korean War started. Since Ray was a corpsman, a nurse, and they needed corpsmen, the military sent him a letter. All of a sudden, Ray was back in the service and on a tanker again in the Pacific.

And then there were the other brothers. Lee came of age, started in the Navy, and ended up working with the Marines. He was on active duty as a corpsman for the Marines in Korea. Dean joined the Air Force for four years.

So I was the last one. And Dad really needed my help on the farm, but I knew that farming wasn't for me. So I reminded Dad that he was in World War I and that my other three brothers went into the military. I told him there was no need for him to try to talk me out of going or do something to stop me because if he went to the draft board, then I would enlist anyway. Everyone else had gone, and I was going to go, too. Dad didn't fight me, even though he needed the help badly. It was going to be hard for him, yet he accepted that. He didn't argue with me or get mad about it. He kind of understood, and it was okay. And that felt really, really good.

I was about to be drafted anyway. The draft board told me that I would go in September or October of 1952, so I enlisted in the Army and became a two-year man. I joined in August of 1952 for two years, figuring I'd be out of the service by August of 1954, in time to get a teacher's job before my five-year certification ran out.

I didn't know it when I went to Fort Leonard Wood in Missouri for basic training, but the foundation of my life was going to be built during that time. I remember an incident that occurred right after I arrived at Fort Leonard Wood. Having lived only on farms in Nebraska for most of my life, I hadn't been exposed to much cultural diversity. But it was the 1950s, and things were starting to change in the area of civil rights in our country. I had just gotten off the bus at Fort Leonard Wood and was in the barracks putting away my clothes. A year or two before, the military had started integrating colored and white—African-Americans and Caucasians. Before that, the African-Americans trained together and the Caucasians trained together, but the two groups did not mix.

Well, in our battalion, we had about half Caucasian and half African-American. When it was chow time, they rang a bell and everybody went over to the mess hall and got in line to get his meal. Anyway, a large African-American was behind me as we were walking. He said to me, "I got just as much right to be in this line as you do." I turned around and saw this big guy, and I said, "I think you do, too." You know, I didn't have any idea what he was talking about at that moment. But it dawned on me as time went by that he'd probably never been in line with a white man before. And he was letting me know that he was in the Army and that he could stand in line with a white man. Not that I was anything special, but I was Caucasian. That was the deal. When you think about that today, it's almost unbelievable—nearly unrecognizable.

After basic training, I completed the Corps of Engineers training. They were tough on us, but they needed to be, and that was okay. I got along well. I was a squad leader and in top physical condition. The strength in my legs and arms was from tossing bales all summer.

Because I had some education and had taught, I had the opportunity to attend the Officers Candidate School (OCS) in Fort Belvoir, Virginia. I had qualified to go and seriously considered doing so, because at that time they needed second lieutenants in the Korean War. You know, they turned out ninety-day wonders—in you came and ninety days later, "poof" you were trained! Then they would send you to Korea. The only catch was that the Army wanted you to sign up for eighteen additional months in the service.

Remember now, at this point I had already met my future wife. She was my fiancée at the time. Lucille asked me some good questions, like, "Do you want to make the Army a career?"

I said, "I don't think so, no."

"Well, then why would you want to stay for eighteen more months?"

And then I thought, "Well, she is smarter than I am, apparently," because I hadn't asked myself that very good question. I just thought that maybe to be an officer would be better than being an enlisted man.

So I went back and told them that I was going to waive my rights to OCS. I didn't know it at the time, but most of the rest of the fellows I trained with went to Korea. The orders had already been sent for the rest of them. They didn't have a place for me to go after I told them I wasn't going to OCS, so they ended up sending me to an electrician school in Fort Leonard Wood. I just moved from one barracks to another barracks and went to electrician school. It was very good training. I learned a lot—from climbing poles to wiring houses—and how to do all kind of things. Then my MOS, that's Military Occupation Service, was 1816 status; I was an electrician.

After completing electrician training, I was one of the fortunate ones that got to go to Europe, not Korea like the rest of them. Some of the guys I trained with got killed over there. Anyway, I had called Lucille before I got my assignment and told her that if I had to go to Korea, I didn't think we should get married because the statistical chance of being killed was much greater than if I was sent to Europe. Fortunately, I was one of the few chosen to go to Europe. So I went home and married my fiancée.

Lucille and I wed on January 24, 1953, at a Lutheran Church in Chappell, Nebraska. That church was plumb full of relatives—hers, mostly. Ray was supposed to be my best man, but he'd come down with jaundice, so my brother-in-law, Kenny Drake, filled in for him. Mother and Dad were there, of course.

Our honeymoon in the States was kind of unusual. During the twenty days I had off after our ceremony, Lucille and I visited family. We went to see two of my sisters and their husbands—Zelma and Ken and Irene and Guy—then spent some time with my folks and some time with her folks. It was a wonderful way to spend time before I shipped to France. That February, Lucille took me to North Platte and put me on the train. I went from there to Camp Kilmer, New Jersey, and then onto a government ship, USS *General R.E. Callan* on its way to Bremerhaven, Germany.

Lucille stayed in Ogallala, Nebraska, to teach until school was out. Then, since we were married, she could join me overseas. Well, she got her passport, jumped on a plane, and flew to Paris because I had recently been assigned to Toul-Rosières Air Base in France. We spent the night in Paris and caught a train back to Pont-à-Mousson, a town near the base, and settled into our little country apartment. We lived in France for fifteen months and just had a great time.

In France, I worked in personnel at the company head-quarters. Stationed as SCARWAF (Special Army with Air Force), I had a very good job with a lot of good people. I was Army but I was assigned to the Air Force. SCARWAF ended up being about half Air Force personnel and half Army personnel. We were engineers there helping put in roads and clear the area for barracks on the base.

Lucille got a job teaching at the school on base. She also cared for the officers' children in the nursery. With her three years of teaching experience, she was qualified. She made twice the money there that she made back in Nebraska. And we could go to work together every day. It just couldn't have worked out any better!

When I first got to France, I bought an old '37 Mercedes Benz, and then later on, Lucille and I bought a new car—an Opel. I paid $1,295 for it through the PX, drove that car 28,000 kilometers all over Europe, and sold it for $1,145. So in my first car business, I lost $150! It got thirty-some miles to the gallon. It was just a little four-cylinder with two seats in the front and two in the back. It was a real good little car, though. We drove that car all over Europe, and we never had a bit of trouble with it.

That first year of our marriage, Lucille and I had a wonderful time in Europe together. We saw fourteen countries in Europe, took pictures, and got to know each other even better while we traveled. That was really our honeymoon. We had that little car, and I had a good job that allowed me to get away. My wife is a Swede so we went to Sweden, of course.

Rome was so interesting to us because of Peter and Paul's experience there. We went to churches and explored the spiritual world of the Catholic Church. And we traveled from the Colosseum to the Appian Way.

We had a good time in England, as well. Through a series of events, we had an opportunity to visit with some folks who lived there, which made it a special deal. See, one day Lucille and I were just a couple of Americans riding on the British underground—the subway—when we started talking to a woman who was riding with us. She ended up inviting us to her house for dinner. Of course, we kind of hesitated. But then her son who had graduated from Oxford and sold tires for Dunlop picked us up from the hotel and took us over to their house. After she fed us, he drove us all around London. We spent a good amount of time with them, just out of the clear blue. I've been back to London many times since then, but it hasn't been the same.

While I was in the military, I developed a lot of deep friendships. We had a great bunch of guys when I was in personnel and lived on Toul-Rosières Air Force Base before Lucille came over. We lived in little huts that the military provided, and, with eight men to a hut, we got to know each other pretty well, pretty fast. After the service, we managed to have a reunion every two years for decades. But there aren't very many left at those reunions anymore.

During my time in Europe, I was an enlisted man, but I spent many of my off-duty hours with officers. This was a little unusual, I guess, but it worked out fine. A couple of those officers turned out to be very influential in my life.

Chaplain Allan, my base chaplain in 1953, was one of them. I admired the fact that he had traveled and could speak several languages. He helped me with my spiritual life and development. My wife played the organ for his chapel services, and I taught Sunday school each week. Lucille and I spent a great deal of time with him and his family, reading the Bible together, praying together, and traveling together. We even stayed with him occasionally when we traveled later on. We frequently visited him and his family after the service. The chaplain is in his nineties now.

Another person who touched my life during my time in the service was a fellow by the name of Rogers. He was a

high-ranking warrant officer and my boss when I was working in personnel. As a warrant officer, he was a man who
had been commissioned up through the ranks and put in
charge of numerous duties. Most warrant officers were very
good soldiers or they wouldn't have even gotten their commission.

In the military, authority meant knowing and following
regulations. And in personnel, we had to know the regulations for everything. Every time we got inspected, Rogers's
expertise and knowledge of the regulations would be challenged. The inspectors would question something or want
to know why we had it that way, and then we would quote
the regulation that supported our decision. Rogers taught
me that if you are going to do something, you had to have
some sort of authority. As long as you knew the regulations,
you were okay. And if you didn't, you were in trouble.

If I had the chance today to hire Rogers, I would put
him in charge of almost anything. He was a very committed,
hard-working man. He was real and humble.

Rogers was probably the most gifted man out of all of
the officers in our company, and not just at work. I learned
that firsthand. See, I used to be pretty good at checkers. In
fact, I could beat most of my brothers at them. Rogers also
had a reputation for being good at chess and checkers, so
one day I sat down to play a game of checkers with him.
Well, I played for ten or so moves. And pretty soon, he said,
"I got ya." And he did. And he won every time after that. I
don't think I ever did beat him.

Rogers also taught me that you need to be organized
and that you need to be up on what you're doing. For in-
stance, if you're trying to become a doctor, you've got to
keep going or you can't achieve or advance. In life, you
have to keep up, you have to keep studying, you have to
keep reading books and learning about different things.

As a supervisor, Rogers also uplifted us any way he
could. He had the gift of helping people wherever they were

to become better. I took that concept with me and brought that into my own professional practices. Sure, I got my degree in teaching, but through the years, I really feel that my true report card has been how well the students, customers, and employees have responded to me.

Part III

Returning Home

For the Lord God is a sun and shield:
the Lord will give grace and glory:
no good thing will he withhold
from them that walk uprightly.
                    —*Psalms 84:11*

5

Getting Down to Business:
Lee Sapp

Helene, the woman who would become my bride, was a wonderful person. I couldn't help falling in love with her when we worked together at the San Diego Naval Hospital. I went overseas while she stayed in California, and I told her, "We're not getting married until I make sure I come back from Korea." She agreed to that. The plan was that I would return to the States, we would both be discharged, and then we would get married.

But there was a glitch in our plan. Helene was a Navy surgery nurse in the tuberculosis unit. Tuberculosis was big back then. Well, Helene herself had come down with tuberculosis while I was overseas. They found it while they were doing the physical so she could be discharged. They took part of her left lung out, but they couldn't discharge her from the military because she still had tuberculosis. She was diagnosed in San Diego, but then they shipped her to a hospital in Corona, California. When I came back to the United States, I was still in the military and was stationed in Chicago.

In 1952, here I was in Chicago with Helene still in California. When I got discharged, I headed home to work on the farm in Odell with Dad for a while. But as soon as I got home, I took his car and headed to California to see Helene for a few weeks. Eventually, I came back and got to work on the farm.

I knew that I needed to get Helene out of California and closer to me as soon as possible, so I reached out to Senator Wherry again and asked for his help. We discovered that the closest hospital for female veterans was in Excelsior Springs, Missouri, right outside of Kansas City. Six months later, Helene was transferred there from Corona, California.

I told Dad, "I'm in love, I want to marry Helene, and I am going to move to Excelsior Springs, Missouri." And I did. I left the farm and went down there. That's where I bought my very first car.

In Excelsior Springs, I got a job at a Ford assembly plant, went to work every day, and lived alone. Back then, they were still building airplanes like they'd done during World War II. But I wasn't in Excelsior Springs with the Ford Motor Company very long, though—just sixty or ninety days at the most.

While I was down in Excelsior Springs, I liked to go to the Masonic Lodge there. One time at the Lodge in 1952, I ran into a banker that I didn't know very well; he was really just an acquaintance. He said to me, "Sapp, how would you like to get in business for yourself, and I'll loan you five thousand dollars? You can just go down to the locker plant and take over the frozen food business there." Needless to say I was pretty surprised. I said, "You know, you're awful nice, but I ain't probably worth five bucks." You see, this man knew me only a little bit through the Masonic Lodge.

It wasn't that I didn't like working at the Ford Motor Company, it was that this guy made me a really good deal. I thought, "There are not too many people that would loan you five thousand dollars or five dollars, for that matter." The truth is that I think that this guy liked me. He thought I was honest and trustworthy.

And that is how I got started in business. I took on the challenge. I said okay, went down, and looked at the place. The one thing that this man didn't tell me, though, was that this frozen food business was going downhill fast. It was going broke! Maybe he thought I could turn the business around. Maybe he thought I'd bring it out of the bad into the good. I'm not sure what he was thinking, but that is exactly what happened.

I think the word got out around the town that my wife-to-be was still up there in the hospital while I was working hard starting up the frozen food business that consisted of a small slaughterhouse and locker plant and just a few customers. I do believe I got business from all sorts of folks who knew about our situation and tried to help us out. We even sold to farmers and city people who wanted to fill their freezers, and that hadn't been done before.

By this point, we knew everybody in the hospital. They had told us that Helene could leave in a certain amount of time, but then when that time came, they said, "No, she isn't quite ready yet." But we told them we were going to go ahead and leave anyway as long as she still had veterans' coverage. She still had to get checked out at the hospital every ninety days or so for quite a few years, however.

So we took off and went to Beatrice, Nebraska, where I had gone to church and school. We were married on October 25, 1953. Her sister flew in from California and was a bridesmaid. And then we went back to Excelsior Springs.

From then on, we were in the frozen food business. I was now the proud owner of Snow Crop of Excelsior Springs. To turn the business around, I called on every restaurant and every business that was serving food. I'd go in and see the owners or managers. I'd talk to them personally. I'd get the orders for the day ahead. Then I got them lined up where I'd deliver the orders on Monday, Tuesday, Wednesday, Thursday, Friday, and Saturday morning. I drove the refrigerated truck. I just started making the rounds.

That is called sales. Without sales, I was nothing. I was very lucky because I got along with people well, and I could joke with them and all that. But I always did it with honesty and integrity, you know. I'd kid around a lot with them; don't misunderstand that. But they knew when I was serious.

And luckily, they bought from me. The people were awfully nice. I don't know what the guy who ran the business before me did that I didn't do or what he didn't do that I did, but the guy in Topeka had the same problem. They had no business there, either. And I turned it around in Topeka when I owned the franchise, and then later on in Omaha. We set a record in Omaha because we were the only ones that ever sold carloads of orange juice to school systems. See, this lady that was in charge of Omaha schools and I thought it'd be good for the students to have orange juice. So we brought in three railroad refrigerated boxcars, put them in storage, and waited for the Omaha School District to pay for it!

After this success, the Snow Crop headquarters down in Florida decided that it would be a good idea for me to go to New York so that their people would buy orange juice, too. So they paid my way to go to New York City for a week. Actually, I didn't stay that long because I was completely out of my environment. Those people didn't want to see a dumb old farm boy come up and shake their hands. One guy said, "Why don't you go back to Nebraska now?" I said, "Thank you. I'm headed back."

So from Excelsior Springs, we moved to Topeka. That's where my son Lee Alan was born in 1957. After living in Topeka for about two years, we moved to Omaha where we raised our family for another three years. Snow Crop headquarters thought I did such a great job there that they wanted me to take the place of a guy who was retiring down in Kansas City. We put a manager, Raymond Morris, who used to work for me down in Topeka up in Omaha. I went down to Kansas City and got the place turned around. All those little towns surrounding Kansas City had to buy through us, see, because we were the regional headquarters and had the regional warehouse. I was probably in Kansas City a couple more years after that. Business was growing and so was our family. Our beautiful daughter, Lori Ann, was born in Kansas City in 1961.

I also helped open up our plant in St. Joe, Missouri; that's where Brother Dean started to work for Snow Crop. In Kansas City, I was in charge of all the operations from Wichita to Columbia. See, I was the owner of Snow Crop franchises in Topeka, Omaha, St. Joe, Kansas City, Wichita, and Jefferson City. I'm thankful to say that every franchise I opened in every location was successful.

After I moved to Kansas City, we brothers used to drive back and forth all the time to see each other. The brothers would come to visit me, and because I was in business for myself, they were real interested in what I was doing. Being your own boss probably sounded pretty good to them. Dean had already worked for me for a while at Kansas City Snow Crop in St. Joe by this time, and Ray had talked Bill into joining him at Prudential Insurance in Nebraska. Eventually, all four of us brothers decided we wanted to get into business together, so I sold out to a company called Fleming, one of the biggest wholesalers in the grocery business at that time. In fact, selling out to Fleming is how I got my share of the investment money to go into business with my brothers in 1960.

But it wasn't easy. As part of the deal, I signed a two-year contract with Fleming. They wanted me to stay with the company, but I kept telling them that I was headed for Nebraska with my brothers.

Now, Ned Fleming was a big shot. He started Fleming & Company, and he was a wonderful, wonderful man. He took me out to lunch often and helped me learn a lot more about business. I already knew that you had to take in more than was going out, but I learned little details from Ned. I knew you had to have a figure in mind every day—what it takes to open the door. And that's business. You may have a deal, but I learned that to make it successful, you've got to do a lot of bidding. I got an education from him, all right, and I was thankful for it.

Every time I would see Ned, I'd say, "You know, I have to go to Nebraska. I have to get back to Nebraska. I'll never be happy with your big company. It's a great company; don't misunderstand. But I'm a Nebraskan. I want to get back to Nebraska because my brothers and I are going to form a company."

"Well," he'd say, "at this time, it's not looking good."

I kept at him for about a year and three months. Every time I'd see him, I'd say, "Can I leave now?" you know, kidding him and stuff like that.

One day later on, Ned Fleming told me, "Sapp, I've been wrong. You can go ahead and leave if you want to." So I took him up on the offer, and we moved back to Omaha in 1962.

What you see is pretty much what you get with all of us brothers. Even though we'd all been in the service for a while, no one seemed any different when we all got back together again. Dean hadn't changed much; Bill hadn't changed much. None of us really changed. Sure, you learn discipline in the military. You know how people get killed in wars, but you didn't have to be there to know that. You do change a little bit, though, as you grow up. That's only natural for anybody.

One of the lessons I learned early on with Snow Crop was that you are no better than the people you hire. Of course, starting the business at Excelsior Springs, I was always the salesperson. Actually, I did a little bit of everything. You had to if you owned the business. But I also had to start managing employees. One was a butcher who'd cut up the meat and the chickens and things like that. Helene even took care of the books down in Excelsior Springs. Then when we started the franchise in Topeka, we had quite a few people working for us.

First, our prospective employees filled out applications. During the first interview, I wouldn't talk very much. The people applying would want to know what their job was going to be like and all that. But I found out their background—if they were born on a farm, how many brothers and sisters they had, and what their work habits were. I didn't hit them all right, but most of them I hired were wonderful people.

Soon after I took over the Kansas City area for Snow Crop Frozen Foods, I was in need of a new secretary. My staff told me that there were five or six ladies waiting to be interviewed in the lobby. I talked to four or five of them, but then I asked if there were any more waiting to be interviewed. I was told that, yes, there was one more, but she didn't have nice clothes on, and she looked real bad. I said over the microphone, "If she's been sitting out there all this time waiting, the least I can do is speak to her and hear her. Send her in. I want to talk to her."

So the gal was sent in. And she was a sad-looking case. I said, "What's wrong with your life?" "Well," she answered, "I just had a baby, and my husband left me." She went on to say, "I haven't got the seventy dollars to get through shorthand school, Mr. Sapp, but if you would loan me the money I'll make you the finest secretary in the world." So I gave her the seventy dollars. Then the other secretary came in and said, "Well, we'll never see her again. She's got her seventy dollars." I said, "Well, probably not, but that's life."

Ninety days or so went by, and then she showed up again. She was wearing a dress made of flour sacks. The woman came into my office and showed me that she'd made it through school. And she said, "Now you've got a job for me, don't you?" Well, I didn't know how good she was or about the school or anything, so we sat around and talked about her family, which was nothing but trouble and more trouble.

So I excused myself and went and talked to another lady in the office. She said, "Well, we really don't need anybody." I said, "We got one person here that isn't working out very well right now." She sure looked shocked when I said that. So we let the other secretary go, and we hired this gal in the flour sacks. Her name was Pat Balvanz. After not too long, we let the other secretaries go and had Pat hire new ones and manage them as the person in charge.

Pat stayed with me for thirty-eight years. It took a lot of guts to do what she did, you know. It was Kansas City in the late 1950s, and she needed the job bad because she just had a baby. And as soon as that baby was born, her husband left her forever.

Pat was always a very loyal employee. Nobody was going to take a nickel out of the pot unless it was approved. That was probably the best seventy bucks I ever invested in my life.

Now I'll tell you something else. When she retired, she brought me a list of all the mistakes I'd made loaning people money and helping people out. On it were the names of all the people I had loaned money to and the amount they never repaid. She'd been holding the complete list all those years. During the course of twenty-eight years, the total unpaid loans reached $2,800,000.

I gave Pat stock in all our companies throughout the years, so she had over three hundred thousand dollars coming out of our stock by the time she retired. She finally had the money to do things, and I was so happy for her. I said, "You know, if you're going to retire, get on a cruise ship and do some of those things you never did." So, she got all of the paperwork ready for the cruise and was all ready to go. But first, she went down and to see her mother in Kansas City in December of 1998. Pat had a cerebral hemorrhage at the Christmas dinner and never got aboard the ship. I was sorry she didn't get a chance to enjoy some of the benefits of all her hard work. Pat knew, though, how much I valued and appreciated her.

I had quite a few good people who worked for me throughout the years. They were very loyal and honest, and they stayed with us for a long, long time. Some stayed with us all of their lives. We grew together professionally and even as friends, and they provided a strong foundation for Sapp Bros.' success, whatever our business.

6

We're Not in Paris Anymore, Lucille: Bill Sapp

Lucille and I had been blessed with a marvelous experience in Europe, but by August of 1954, it was time to come home. We had been able to save some money in Europe, so when we got back in the United States, we bought a brand new Ford and paid for it in full. We picked it up right from the dealer in New York and drove that car all the way back to Nebraska.

Back in the States, Lucille and I both were fortunate enough to get teaching positions in the small town of Franklin, Nebraska. Lucille's sister helped us by telling the school superintendent, Ken Willits, about our qualifications and our desire to teach there. She must have done a great job promoting us because the superintendent hired us sight unseen! We had a really nice time teaching there for two years. I taught math and social studies and coached football, basketball, and track for Franklin Junior High School and was also the elementary school principal.

I kept everything real simple when I was coaching football. We usually ran the ball and passed only a few times during a game. But we usually won. My boys weren't too big, but they were fast and talented.

I remember one time our football team was playing Alma—a junior high school up the road. Alma had a real big boy who was pretty strong and fast. He was a little older—an eighth grader, I think. I was dealing with a bunch of younger boys on my team, and I knew we didn't have enough players to stop him. Funny thing was, they couldn't stop us either because we could outrun them. Every time they'd get the ball, they made a touchdown. Then, we'd get the ball, and we'd make a touchdown. At half-time, the score was fourteen to fourteen.

During the half-time. I told them, "Once you get to them, grab them wherever you can and hang on. If you get the big guy, the others have to come and help you. If they don't, he's going to get away, and we're going to lose."

I said, "It's up to you to grab him and hang on until the others get there. And you other guys must run as fast as you can and help because that guy is big, and he can carry a couple of you along the way."

Then I added, "Now you've got to make up your mind to win this game or you know what's going to happen. They can't stop us if you guys don't let them. They can't get to us. We're going to outplay them all, but you've got to stop that guy."

My boys went back on the field for the second half of the game. We scored once more, and the other team didn't score once during the entire last half.

I told the kids what the problem was and explained what the solution was. And it worked. If you just tell them what the problem is, they don't always understand how to find the solution, so nothing improves. I tried to inspire them and relied on the respect they had for me. And they had talent. With that combination of elements, all of the teams I coached did well, and we beat most of the other schools. After I had moved on from teaching years later, it was fun to watch these same kids compete in state football, basketball, and track competitions. A lot of them did very well in high school sports.

I enjoyed teaching, but in August 1956, I left teaching; we moved from Franklin to Lincoln, so I could continue studying mathematics at the University of Nebraska at Lincoln.

The soldiers that came back from World War II were granted a wonderful opportunity to continue their education with the G.I. bill. Brother Ray completed his schooling through that bill. After my time in the service, I was able to follow in his footsteps.

Luckily, Lucille had saved six hundred dollars out of her teaching paychecks during the previous two years, so we could go look for a house in Lincoln. We needed to find a house pronto because we already had one baby and were about to have another.

By the grace of God, our real estate agent found us a duplex at 1235 New Hampshire, which is right across the tracks from the University of Nebraska. In fact, you could see the whole university campus out of our back window.

Now this wasn't an actual duplex; it was a house made into a duplex. One unit was the first floor, and the other unit was in the basement. The previous owners had renovated the basement and made an apartment for their parents. They had the bathroom, bedroom, and living room all fixed up in knotty pine. It was a good thing we found it, because pretty soon Lucile and I had a whole house full of girls—our three daughters: Suzanne, Nancy, Mary.

When the previous owner's parents had passed away, they put their house up for sale. Then we came along. They were in the process of buying a new home in Lincoln somewhere. They were selling on contract. We had our $600 dollars, so we gave it to them, and they sold us the house. I think we paid about $86 a month for our house payment, and that included the principal, taxes, and insurance. And we rented out the basement to college students for $55 a month. The whole time we lived there, our house payment was only $31 a month out of pocket! And that was just wonderful, you know, because Lucille couldn't work, having the three babies and all, and I was back at school. Then I got a job at the *Lincoln Journal Star* and supervised ninety-six paperboys in southeast Lincoln. I worked thirty to seventy hours a week because I took the morning route from 4:00 to 6:00 A.M. three times a week and then worked the evening routes. We got a base pay plus so much for mileage on our cars, so I got gas money.

It was a great job because I could work the hours I wanted to. The *Journal Star* encouraged people in my position to work with the carriers as many hours as they could. When I was on Christmas or spring break, I could substitute for other supervisors and make extra money. I also sometimes wrote articles for the paper. Lucille cared for some of the neighbors' kids as well as ours, so that helped our financial situation, too.

I got into the real estate business house by house. One day, I was out in my backyard when I noticed some people looking at the neighboring house. I said, "What are you doing?" They told me, "Oh, we own this house. We can't rent it out anymore, so we want to sell it." I asked them how much they wanted for it and told them if they'd sell it on contract, I would buy it. And they said, "We'll do that." So I bought the house next door.

Then I bought another duplex on South 24th. After that, one of the guys that I was going to school with was in crisis and had a trailer house on West O that he had to sell. I bought that one real cheap. Then, later on in '58 or '59, Ray and I decided to buy a six-plex together. We found one that was real old and in bad shape, and we fixed it up. Ray and I worked on that place day and night. To renovate all these houses, I relied on what I'd learned from moving around so often as a kid. All that painting and wallpapering we were always doing on the farm came in real handy. I could fix anything I put my mind to.

I finally graduated from the University of Nebraska at Lincoln in 1958 and learned Stromsburg High had an opening for a math teacher and a coach. This was good news because jobs usually weren't available midterm. I'd had some coaching experience by then, and I majored in math in college, so I decided to turn in my application.

But then there was Ray, who was in a leadership role for Prudential Insurance Company. See, Ray studied animal husbandry in college, went to work for Goodrich, and then moved to the Quad Cities. Lenora, Ray's wife, had been raised in the Beatrice and Lincoln area, and she didn't like living in the Quad Cities at all. She persuaded him to leave there and come back to Nebraska. So Ray came back and got a job with Prudential Insurance Company.

Now, growing up, Ray was always a great buddy of mine. He and I were usually partners when we played games with Lee and Dean. Now he wanted me to come and sell insurance with him.

I said, "Ray, I can't sell insurance." And he said, "Well, Bill, I think you can, and you'll make twice as much as you can teaching." He assured me that he would not be my boss and pointed out that I already lived here in town, already had the basement income and other income from the houses, and already was living reasonably well. He said, "You come on and try this, and if you don't like it, you can always quit." So I decided to give it a shot.

Ray got me the job, but, like he said, I didn't work for him. Sure, he helped me out by giving me some leads, but it was much better for me to be the one going out on calls, so I could learn the ropes. My boss was actually a guy by the name of Walt Nicholson. Both Ray and Walt were assistant managers at Prudential; their title was like one in the Army—sergeant first class. Ray was quickly moving up the ladder at that time because he had been with the company for quite a while and had the experience. So Ray was above me in seniority and experience. He was a staff manager, and I was what they called an agent.

I went to work for Prudential Life Insurance Company in January of '59, and I did very well. I had gotten my bachelor's degree from University of Nebraska, but I got a master's degree in selling from Prudential without the certificate because they had a great training program for their agents. Each Friday we had classes. They trained us to sell.

The company also wanted to give incentives to all their agents to achieve, so they listed weekly what each agent had sold. This technique worked well with me because I was very competitive and wanted to be recognized. I think the message they were trying to get across to all of us was this: "If others can do well, you can too!" The strategy was meant to encourage the agents to try hard, and they'd give out prizes to those who did well. In fact, I won the agent's trip to New Orleans to attend the national sales convention, so Lucille and I got to go down there. She was pregnant with Cindy, our last daughter, then. Those prizes were a real catalyst for incentive. Anyway, I worked hard up until I quit Prudential in June of 1960 to go into business with my brothers.

How we Sapp brothers got into business together was an interesting turn of events. It all started in 1960 when Brother Lee, who was living in Kansas City, came up to Lincoln to visit Ray and me. He also spent some time with his former neighbor, Jess Carraway, a guy who worked for a Ford dealership in Omaha. We all got to talking and decided that the four of us brothers would buy the Ford dealership in Ashland, Nebraska.

Looking back, I see how all my experiences leading up to the Sapp Bros. prepared me for this new career. I think the service was great for me because of the special lessons I learned there. My experience teaching school also was valuable, as were the business practices I learned from buying those old houses. And working for Prudential was really the catalyst I needed to push me into sales; without my time at Prudential, I would have had no confidence in my ability to sell anything to anyone.

If I'd have gone from teaching directly into the car business, I don't know if we'd have made it. But I went from teaching right to Prudential where they taught me to sell. And if I could sell an insurance policy, which is completely intangible, selling a car you can actually see and touch wasn't such a leap. Prudential had taught me a lot about how to sell and who is going to buy a product. When you're trying to sell a car, you've got to figure out what the customer really wants and what questions to ask.

Ray and I both brought our experience selling insurance to the car dealership. At Prudential, we learned that when you are trying to sell something, you have to know your product, stay positive, and have confidence. You have to listen to the customer. Find out what he needs, find out what he wants—not what you want for him—and then you sell to that.

After my brothers and I decided to go into business together, I needed to put my financial share into the dealership. Turns out it was pretty easy for me to raise my fourth of the investment because I still had all of those houses. I sold them all, and I made good money off them. That wasn't because I was so gifted and smart; it was simply inflation. Anything that you bought back in '56 or '57 was worth more money in '60, but I had nothing to do with that!

Part IV

Joining Forces: The Sapp Bros.

For I mean not that other men be eased,
and ye burdened: But by an equality,
that now at this time your abundance may be a supply
for their want, that their abundance
also may be a supply for your want:
that there may be equality:
—II Corinthians 8:13, 14

7

Coming Together, Working It Out: Lee Sapp

On June 1, 1960, we four Sapp brothers banded together to become Sapp Bros. Ford Sales, Inc. in Ashland, Nebraska, and opened the doors of our first business.

The idea of the four of us going into business together started when I was working for Snow Crop in Kansas City during the late 1950s. My brothers wanted to get into business for themselves like I was. What that business would be, we had no idea. Then I remembered a neighbor I had had in Omaha who worked for Ford Motor Company. Jess Carraway was his name and we were good friends back in those days.

Because Jess had been with Ford Motor Company for a while, he knew what the Ford dealers were doing and what was going on. So, when the brothers came down to Kansas City and started talking to me about all of us going into business, I said, "Well, I think we might be able to get a Ford dealership through Jess Carraway." Turns out Jess Carraway was the one who lined everything up for us, and we bought out the Andrews brothers on June 1, 1960. Each of us brothers had agreed to come up with ten thousand dollars, one-fourth of the money we needed to invest in the dealership.

Once we opened our doors for business on that lovely June day, the only real problem was that none of us had any actual experience selling cars. Ford didn't especially care for that fact when they found out about it. See, Jess had lawfully approved everything in Nebraska to make the deal go through, but Ford became aware of our situation only later on when the paperwork finally made its way up to Detroit.

Ford Motor Company came back and told us that we couldn't continue to own the dealership because none of us had any experience selling cars. They figured because we had no experience we weren't going to make it. But it was way too late! We probably had already sold more cars in the short time we had been open than the previous dealership had in three years, and we were doing more business than the biggest dealership in Lincoln, if that tells you anything. We sold to people from Ashland, Lincoln, Omaha, you name it. So Jess showed Ford the statistics and how much money we had already made. The Ford manager out of Omaha even flew into Detroit and said, "You people are crazy for wanting to shut these guys down! They're selling cars like hotcakes!" After learning this, headquarters was happy to approve us, and that's how Sapp Bros. got started.

Because Dean and I had some unfinished business in the Kansas City area, Bill and Ray were the ones who ran the dealership in Ashland at first. They made sure they treated all the customers nice and friendly. And they worked hard, to put it mildly. Bill and Ray started at 5:00 or 6:00 in the morning and stayed until 8:00 or 9:00 at night.

I wasn't able to move back from Kansas City right away because part of the agreement I made in selling out to Fleming in 1960 was that I would continue to work for them in Kansas City for a while longer. Those first couple of years down in Kansas City, though, I made sure to buy all of our Snow Crop cars and trucks from the Ashland dealership. In three more years, we were all back together again going full speed ahead.

Another venture of ours was buying some land in Blair in 1963 and building another car dealership on it. There was nothing on it when we bought that land. Dean got the business up and running successfully and later Ray would join him after the Ashland dealership was sold. The two of them did a great job of running that dealership together, even though all four of us owned it.

By 1965, Sapp Bros. had acquired another dealership—a GMC truck dealership in Omaha this time. Bill and I ran that one together, just the two of us. I'd stay there until 1972.

Now don't get me wrong, we brothers didn't always agree—especially when it came to business decisions. Brothers and sisters argue once in a while; they can't agree on everything. I think we probably weren't as bad as some families I've heard of, but I'm not sure of that. Our hardship, the Depression, and the way we grew up kind of forced us together. Growing up, we were a normal family, but we just didn't have any money.

When we became the Sapp Bros., if there was a dispute over a business deal among us, we would put it to a vote. Because there were four of us, though, you can imagine that the vote often turned out to be two against two. With four of us, see, there was no tie breaker. So, the deal was that if two of us agreed and two of us disagreed, we usually would just not do whatever it was that was up in the air. When it went three in favor and one against, then we did it—the majority ruled. Usually, the one person who had voted against the others was pretty cooperative in the end. Oh, I'm not telling you that there weren't times we'd be talking about a deal over refreshments and somebody would say, "I know you three are wrong, but you won't admit it." You know, just kidding around. That definitely happened. Once in a while, one of us brothers would even try to swing the vote of the others.

When you're in business, it's got to be a two-way street. But if you have your money in it, it feels like it's all yours, instead of just a fourth yours. That's why we relied so heavily on the voting system. I wasn't always right, Ray wasn't always right, Dean wasn't always right, and Bill wasn't always right. But that's the best part of it. There was safety in numbers. Teamwork was very important to us all individually, and it was a huge factor in our success as a whole. Bill was forever saying, "We did it together"; "It was teamwork"; "If I did something, I'd check with the brothers." His attitude was the attitude we all had.

We didn't talk very much to Mom and Dad about business issues because there was no sense in burdening them with hypothetical problems that might never become reality. Also, it would have been hard for them to be objective when the brothers disagreed. See, I was still in the food business and supplying Mom and Dad with food. That could make them lean my way, which wouldn't have been fair.

Each of us brothers was humble. That was a strength we each brought to the table when we joined forces in 1960. We all were pretty equal in that we didn't have very much money. We all were married and raising kids at the time, and when you are trying to raise a family, you don't have very much financial stability.

We all brought experience to Sapp Bros., but we all offered something different. I think our differences made us stronger, though, because if you've got two people who think alike, you don't need one of them. Luckily, we were a pretty well-rounded group by the time we all came together in 1960.

People liked Ray like people like dogs. Ray was an honest and a likable guy, and if you have those two things, it is always good for sales. If people trust you, you can sell. Being so likable made him a great salesman. You know if a person tells you the truth with integrity and he smiles and jokes, you normally like the guy. And Ray was that way naturally. While we were growing up, whenever anyone got to know Brother Ray—through playing cards or dancing or whatever—that person would tell me, "Boy, I sure do like your brother, Ray." Ray was not very mechanically minded, but he could do paperwork as well as sell. He also was a good thinker, and his vote was always very important. The biggest strength Ray brought to the business was his good, consistent salesmanship.

Now Dean, on the other hand, was more serious, but he was born with a lot of mechanical talent. And he was a fair salesperson, as well, in my opinion. He was also a very hard worker.

Bill was more astute and was good with bookkeeping. And he and Ray both had a lot of sales experience from working together at Prudential.

I'm the only brother without a college education. Ray and Bill both graduated from the University of Nebraska at Lincoln, and Dean went for two years to a college in Topeka. Luckily, I had some sales experience to offer the group. My brothers used to tease me that I could sell ice cubes to Eskimos.

A big part of Sapp Bros.' success has been our dedicated employees. You have to have good help. Our employees have been wonderful and extremely loyal. We have several employees at our truck stops, in our petroleum company, and just about everywhere, who are in their seventies and getting close to eighty. You pretty near have to run them out to get rid of them! They own stock and are pretty well off nowadays. Our people stay with us.

Allen Marsh, our chief financial officer, is a good example of a solid employee who has stuck with us for a long,

long time. He worked for the CPA firm that used to audit us when we first got started. We kind of liked Allen back then, and then one day, he just came out and said, "Why don't you guys hire me?" So we did. He should be retired by now, but he isn't. Allen is a good man. He's been Sapp-brainwashed—a great asset to us!

Another employee who was a standout was Al Kent. He loved to sell. Anything. Even if there wasn't much money in it for him, he would make the sale just for fun. He was in Ashland and would just sell people. Everybody liked him. He was a tremendous salesman. We've had a lot of terrific salespeople over the years.

Some people have asked us how we brothers got so good at sales. My answer is that we're honest, we like people, and God helped us. We also had a lot of friends and acquaintances from all the small towns we lived in growing up who came and bought cars from us. They'd all stop in at our truck stop and eat because they knew us Sapp brothers when we were their neighbors.

Because all of us brothers turned out to be pretty good salespeople, each of us won several vacations through Ford Motor Company and General Motors. I won trips to Uganda and Spain. Bill, Dean, and Ray all won a lot of trips, too.

I attribute a lot of our early success to our being honest and trustworthy. That's how we went from Ashland to Blair to GMC to the truck stops to petroleum, and right on down the line. But a lot of our success was also timing and the economy. We had nothing to do with those things. We acquired a lot of land that people talked us into buying because it was adjacent to ours. And what better thing could you own but land? God isn't making any more land. And our land has made us more money on the dollar, percentage-wise, than anything we ever did, except maybe the oil business now.

Other factors that contributed to our success over the years were positive thinking and faith in God. During the early days, especially, I remember turning to God for guidance several times. We just had to trust in God that everything would work out if we were doing right by others. And it did.

See, we were building our business back then. As we grew, we didn't hit a home run every time we got up to bat, and it took awhile to experience success. But we didn't ever give up, and we took one step at a time. We got on first, then made it to second, then went on to third, and then sometimes we made it home. If you want to think negative, you're going to go negative. You've got to think positive.

Believe me, the road wasn't always smooth, but when it came to sales, perseverance paid off for us. I remember one time, the guy in charge of fleet cars at Union Pacific threw me out of his office. He said, "We don't buy GMC. You're wasting your time, and you're wasting my time. Get the hell out!" So I called the president of Union Pacific and filled him in. I said, "I'm not asking you to buy from me, but give me a chance, and I think you'll find that our product and our salesmanship will compete with anybody's." In ninety days, Union Pacific was buying GMC trucks from me. Pretty soon, in Omaha we had not only Union Pacific, but also Fairmont Foods, Kitty Clover, Coca-Cola, Peter Kiewit, Hawkins, Mutual of Omaha, and the state buying cars and trucks from us. They all didn't play as hard to get as Union Pacific, though.

See, we sold at cost plus. It was an idea that Bill and I came up with. Whatever the car or truck cost from the manufacturer, we would add so many dollars and cents to that, and that would be the price of the vehicle. Every time a company bought a car or a truck, I would give them a copy of the manufacturer's invoice showing our cost. Although we offered to let them, we never got audited by one of those companies—not by a one.

Now, most dealers don't show customers the paperwork that comes to them; they try to fool their customers instead. But to me, there's no sense in trying to fool them because customers are pretty smart people. I made sure the companies buying from us had every invoice made out to Sapp Bros. If they wanted us to, we'd even back that invoice up with the check we wrote to General Motors. It was a brand-new idea; nobody else had thought of it. And the customers loved it. We didn't charge a whole lot above our cost, and we worked on volume.

We were the only GMC truck dealer around that sold over-the-road trucks, and one year using that method we even outsold the Chicago and Kansas City dealerships, according to General Motors. Another factor in our success was that we went the extra mile for our customers. If a couple had trouble with their car, and the warranty didn't cover it, sometimes we'd go ahead and cover what the customer thought Ford or General Motors should've covered. Not always, but sometimes. It depended on the predicament; it depended a lot on how the couple was doing. We tried to help people who were struggling. We always tried to help the underdog, because we were underdogs for a long time. And that is something you never forget.

As far as strategic planning went, well, our plans really depended on the money that was coming in. If you don't have money coming in, then you've got to watch the economy. If people aren't buying cars and trucks very fast, then it's not a time to build your inventory. Most of good business sense is common sense, really.

Every day on the hour, people's desires and dreams get ahead of them in business, and they try to do too much too fast. But we never thought that way. We just keep working and trying to do better. I always just counted my blessings. Every day you should count your blessings, because you don't have to look very far to see somebody worse off.

Sapp Bros., just like any business that has been around for a while, has seen its share of hard times, good times, and bad times. We've had our ups and our downs. The '80s were some tough years, but we got through them.

God didn't make any of us perfect, and we all have made mistakes. We certainly made mistakes in our business. There is no doubt about that. But if you focus on honesty, integrity, and serving God by helping your fellow man, you're going to make it.

8

Learning as We Go: Bill Sapp

Who would have thought that fewer than two years after graduating from college, I'd be buying a car dealership with my brothers? Before I knew it, we were growing so fast we also had a Ford dealership in Blair and a GMC franchise in Omaha. Lee's former neighbor in Omaha, Jess Carraway, worked for Ford Motor Company and mentioned to Lee that it wouldn't take much money to buy a very good Ford dealership in Ashland, Nebraska, and maybe we should consider buying it. When Lee brought it up to us, we thought, "Well, this could be the opportunity we've been hoping for! It sounds like a good deal. Let's give it a college try!"

The dealership in Ashland was owned by three older gentlemen—Charlie Andrews who was a banker in Syracuse, his brother Brett, and another individual. Brett and Charlie's partner was dying of cancer, and the brothers recognized it would be in the best interest of the man's family and the business if the dealership could be sold before he passed on. So, we hurried to Ashland to see the three men, made them an offer, and bought the dealership from them in June of 1960. The Ford Omaha office approved us, but the headquarters in Detroit had not approved the deal. Each brother owned a fourth of the dealership because each one had raised his quarter of the forty thousand dollars needed.

Since we had bought out the Andrews brothers and their partner and taken over the dealership in Ashland as Sapp Bros. Ford Sales, Inc., we had a number of new cars, but not too many at that time because back in the 1960s, June was a month for gearing down in the new car business. In August, Ford stopped making the current year's model, and in September and October the brand new models came out, looking very different from those of the previous year.

We were all so excited to be doing business together. Ray and I were the ones who actually ran the dealership. The previous owners had been renting the building from the bank, so we followed suit. We got commercial credit to finance the cars that we sold.

Ray and I both moved during the summer of 1960 to Ashland and found it to be a great little town. From the Ford dealership, we could look right down the main street of Ashland.

When Ray and I went to work at the dealership, we had two salesmen at first, but one wasn't very good and he was soon gone. Then it was just the three of us—Brother Ray, Al Kent, and me. We all sold cars and we did quite well.

A few months later, however, Ford told us we were not approved by Detroit to own and operate the dealership. Apparently, they finally determined we were not qualified for three reasons: we were too young, we had no previous business experience, and we didn't have enough cash.

Well, we already had bought the dealership. With Jess Carraway's encouragement, the division office in Omaha had approved us and forwarded our names to Detroit as owners of a new dealership in Ashland, Nebraska.

Recognizing that, Ford came back to us and said, "Well, we'll let you go until you go broke. You're not going to make it, though, for the three reasons we mentioned before." They sounded like a broken record.

Ford did come around in a pretty short time, though. Although we hadn't been in business very long, we had sold quite a few cars by the time the Ford representative came down to check things out. They changed the way they looked at us when they saw our numbers and realized how many cars and trucks we were selling and how quickly we were moving them. We were selling them very competitively and following through on every lead.

The dealers in Omaha and Lincoln, however, were really perturbed with us. Here was this little car dealer out there messing up the market and selling cars too cheap. We could sell cars for less money than they could because we didn't have near the fixed overhead that they did. They had sales managers and owners, and we *were* the sales managers and owners and everything else in between.

Although none of us had any prior experience selling cars, Ray and I had sold insurance, and because we were successful selling insurance, we were successful selling cars. Part of our early success in selling cars in Ashland came because we were very hard workers. We sold a lot of cars at night. People would come to us in the evening right after they got off work. We were there all the time for them. We were open six days a week from 6:00 A.M. to 9:00 P.M. Monday through Saturday. One of us was always there—usually both. Evening hours were very important to our success. In fact, we probably delivered more cars at night than at any other time. If we weren't selling cars, we were cleaning up the ones we had taken for trade during the day.

During the month of June 1961, one year after we opened, Ray, Al Kent, and I sold 300 cars among the three of us—100 new ones and 200 used ones. That's an average of about 10 cars a day. Our incredible sales record was due in large part to our great salesman, Al, who just loved to sell cars. He had worked for the Andrews brothers before we bought them out, but he really hit his stride working for us. He couldn't work for anybody else by then, though, because he broke all the rules. Al would go anywhere and do anything to sell a car. He'd say, "I'll sell it; I'll work it out." And then he did. And he did a lot of "creative" things, shall we say. And then some of the things he did were just plain stupid, but we all do stupid things. He'd say to Ray and me, "I'll make it work somehow, even if it takes several deals to do it!"

He called us brothers "the boys" and never fussed with any of us. He seemed happy with the deal we struck with him—we furnished him with a car and paid for all his gas and expenses, and he got 25 percent of whatever we made. So if we made $200, he made $50 dollars. And if we got $400, then he made $100. If we made nothing, he got nothing. He was on straight commission plus expenses. He sold a great number of cars over the years, but on some he never made a dime. However, at the end of the year, the income on his W-2 form was much higher than ours because we worked for a straight salary.

In those days, we took almost anything in for trade, and I think that helped people get into one of our cars. We traded for combines, trucks, and cattle, as well as for used cars. We even traded for a beach house in South Bend and an old Model T up on ropes in a garage! We got a reputation for being willing to look at almost anything a potential buyer might want to trade.

The three of us sold so many cars and trucks that we often got bonuses from Ford Motor Company. And every year, Al was the outstanding salesman for Ford Motor Company because of the number of cars he sold. He was a great salesman and a big help to both Ray and me during those early days. We sold a lot of cars there in Ashland with Al's help. After a couple of years, the dealership was doing very well. We were doing so well, in fact, that we were number one among Ford dealerships our size. We were pretty young and inexperienced back then, but every year we were at Ashland, we made a lot more than we paid ourselves.

❦------------❦

Ford came to us and said, "Well, we have a dealership in Broken Bow, Nebraska, and we are wondering if you would like to buy it." We went up to Broken Bow way up in central Nebraska and quite a ways north. It's a small, nice little town. But it's cattle and ranch country up there, and they don't buy many cars. Even if everybody in the area would buy a Ford car—and everybody *wouldn't* buy a Ford car—you wouldn't sell nearly as many as we were selling in Ashland. If a guy wanted to retire and run a small dealership out there, he could make some money, but for our purposes, it wasn't quite right. So, we turned Ford down.

Later, Ford offered us a dealership in Blair, Nebraska. Ray and I went up to Blair to check the situation out and wound up purchasing thirteen acres. Part of the deal was that the man who originally owned the land could remain living in the house on the property until he passed away.

Ray had some friends in Lincoln who were contractors, so we asked them to bid on building a car dealership for us on this land. Don Fry, a friend of ours, designed it and, in fact, eventually designed most of our travel centers.

Dean decided to take on the Blair dealership. The only problem was that Dean really didn't have a lot of experience with that kind of thing. But he came to Ashland for a while to see what we did and then worked with us there for a period of time, before Blair opened, to get his feet wet and see what would be expected of him.

Because all four of us owned both of the dealerships, we used a lot of our cash flow, people, and used cars from Ashland to get Blair off the ground. Our parts man even went up there and worked with their parts man. We had a lot of our people in Ashland going back and forth to Blair for a good while.

The older gentleman who sold us the land and lived in the house on the property died before we even opened the door to the Blair dealership. I think Dean and his wife, Susie, moved into his house for a time while their new home on the hill was being built. Then they sold the old house and it got moved off of our property to a spot a short distance away.

After we were in business for a while, the state bought some of our property on Highway 30 to widen it so they could get more lanes there. The state paid us little money because they used just a small part of our land. The best we ever got out of those deals were entryways to our dealership. And actually, they were more valuable to us than any money we received from the state.

The success of the Blair dealership was due mostly to Dean's hard work. Of the four of us, he was the hardest worker. I'm a hard worker, too, but Dean was a workaholic. He was at the dealership at the crack of dawn and worked late into the evenings. Dean hired some great salesmen, too, and as a result of his hard work and theirs, the dealership did very well. So now we had two car dealerships—one in Ashland and one in Blair—that were very successful.

Over time, though, Ford put us on a ration of cars. It was our impression that they did this to satisfy the big dealers in Lincoln and Omaha who felt they were losing sales because of us. We didn't have the big overhead they did, so of course we could be very competitive in our pricing. The bigger dealerships, however, felt they were turning into service dealerships; in other words, people would drive to Ashland to buy cars from us and then use their local dealerships only when they needed their cars serviced. Ford probably felt their rationing policy toward us would level the playing field, but it didn't seem fair to us. We could get only so many cars at a time, and then we'd have to wait months to get more. Some of our customers didn't want to wait months for their new cars, so that was a problem.

Because of our difficulties with Ford, we jumped at the opportunity when a GMC truck dealership came up for sale in Omaha in 1965. We thought we could handle it because we had handled Blair. We looked at the numbers and figured we could manage it well enough with the success of the other two dealerships we had up and running. We planned to take capital out of Blair and Ashland to buy the new trucks and new equipment, and train people for the new GMC truck dealership. Now remember, technically, we did not have enough capital back in 1960 to open the Ashland dealership. But then we did well enough to buy land and a building in Blair and buy this truck dealership in Omaha, so we felt confident we could make this new venture work, as well.

At that time, Ray was in Ashland and Dean was in Blair, so all the brothers decided that I should go to Omaha to run the new GMC truck dealership. I knew a few things about trucks from selling Ford trucks, although at our other dealerships we sold mostly farm trucks, not the over-the-road trucks. At the time we purchased the GMC truck dealership, I lived in Ashland, so I had to drive to Omaha each day.

We opened the doors to GMC Trucks of Omaha in 1965 while we still owned the Ashland and Blair dealerships, so suddenly we were juggling three dealerships at once.

The GMC garage located at 11th and Pierce Street was part of the old Omaha streetcar building, which was a very good facility for us in a lot of ways. When the city discontinued the use of streetcars, the old Omaha streetcar barn was leased or sold to someone else. We rented the top floor of the two-story building.

Soon we learned that the words Ford Motor Company spoke to us back in 1960 were true: it does take a lot of capital to succeed in this business. We came to understand this fact through the school of hard knocks.

We figured that because we had grown and made enough money in Ashland and Blair, we could just keep going. We had kept our overhead low, and we did a lot of the work ourselves. We worked long, hard hours. In Blair, Dean was the sales manager, the owner, and everything else, and Ray and I were the same, in our respective locations.

But pretty soon, we all discovered that we were growing too fast. We were running three dealerships within just five years. But just as we had experienced in the beginning, we found we did not have enough cash flow.

We all knew we were hurting. We had to do something. In the truck business we soon ran out of cash, even after taking out bank loans to increase our capital. It took a lot more money to survive and thrive in the truck business than in the car business because we were dealing with truckers buying multiple trucks or a fleet of them, not just an individual buying a single car. And then we had to pay GMC a few days after delivery. Because we needed the cash almost immediately, that created a cash flow problem.

At some point, we realized that we weren't going to be able to run that truck dealership with the money we had; we agreed we needed more capital, plain and simple. As a group we decided the simplest way to get it would be to sell the Ashland dealership. Ray would then move to Blair to help Dean. It was pretty obvious that we had gotten too big for our britches. That was the sad truth of the matter. Ashland was home ground for us, but we needed to move on.

We sold the Ashland dealership to Ron Grebe and his business partner, Marv Ficken, and put the money into GMC Trucks. We took all the cars, inventory, parts, and cash receivables and used them to strengthen the Blair and Omaha dealerships.

Selling Ashland proved to be a good decision in the end. Later on, Lee and his son would buy the dealership back when Grebe needed to sell. Lee arranged for Ron to continue to work up in Ashland at the dealership for a little while, which seemed to work out very well for both of them.

After Ashland closed in 1965, Ray made some big sacrifices. To build up our cash flow, which was very important, Ray sold his house, bought another house, moved his family from Ashland to Blair, and then came in as second fiddle working at the Blair dealership with Dean. Dean had been running the Blair dealership singlehandedly and successfully for about three years at that point. Ray had been running the dealership in Ashland. So, needless to say, there was a little friction there. Not a lot, but a little.

Starting up a dealership is a pretty good-sized undertaking. To get it all put together, get everything arranged and designed, and up and going takes a lot of different skills. And just as important is getting good people to run the place and follow through. It takes all of these things to make a business work properly.

Each of us brothers had his strengths. Lee was able to open up some doors that we probably wouldn't have been able to walk through otherwise. In all fairness, I would say that Lee was by far the best salesman of the four of us. I am more analytical than Lee, but he could sure sell people. Lee was just a natural because he is very likable. He has a great personality. He likes people. He is Mr. Congeniality—he does a great job of meeting people and being cordial to them. That's his strength.

Brother Ray's biggest contribution to Sapp Bros. was to help us see the total picture. He was very positive and kind to each of us and was a good salesman, too. He was the oldest brother, so he was the one that we each would ask how we should approach things. Ray's strength was to help; he was always willing to do his share of the work. In fact, he went overboard to do his share. He really contributed to our business running smoothly because he would do whatever it took to soften and smooth the edges. Ray was a strong team player, as we all were, but some of us, including me, were bent on doing things our way at times.

Ray may have been the most giving brother, as far as working and doing to help the cause. He was the one who gave up his comfort zone and moved more than the rest of us.

Ray and I worked really well together because he would help me set my plans in motion. I was usually the guy with the ideas—you know, "Let's do this!" and "Let's try this!" And then Ray would be the one who would tell the brothers, "Well, Bill wants to try this." And then we'd do it. He was very supportive.

Dean, on the other hand, was kind of a go-between among the four of us and would balance everything out. He was good at working closely with Lee and was the brother who kept us in harmony and balance. And that was very important, obviously. As I said, Dean was a very hard worker—probably the hardest worker of us all. He really poured his heart and soul into running the Ford dealership in Blair. He was incredibly committed to that project and spent a lot of hours down there. Dean worked so much that his wife, Susie, had to find other things to do, like volunteer at church or go bowling. Fortunately, Susie was a farm girl and liked living the farming lifestyle. She found enough time to build a barn and tend to some horses and cattle while Dean worked sixty or more hours a week down at that dealership.

My biggest contribution to the group was probably managing, controlling situations, and just keeping things going.

All the brothers' contributions were important, and all the brothers did their share. The four of us were partners in everything. When we first started Sapp Bros., it was 25 percent per brother for everything, and that is how it stayed. That's the way it was for the dealerships in Ashland, Blair, and Omaha. Learning how to work together was an essential part of our success as the Sapp Bros.

Part V

Growing the Family

All things were made by Him;
and without Him was not any thing made
that was made. In Him was life;
and the life was the light of men.
                    —*John 1:3, 4*

9

Life's Treasures: My Helene, Peanut, and Lee Alan: Lee Sapp

We had a great family—my wife, our two kids, and me. If you saw one of us, you saw all of us.

Helene and I couldn't start a family right away because of her health, but the wait was worth it. We had our son, Lee Alan, in Topeka in 1957 and Lori Ann in Kansas City four years later. Fortunately by then, our Snow Crop frozen food business was doing well, so we'd started making some money.

Both of our kids were outstanding students. No doubt about that. They got their brains from their mother. You can't have college degrees and be successful like they've been and not have some smarts about you.

Although, as I said, we were doing pretty well financially by the time our children came along, Helene and I made sure they were disciplined. I was very strict with them, and I think that helped them tremendously. We had conversations about life's dos and don'ts and just really communicated. I could afford to give them things at that point, but I didn't give them everything they wanted.

I made my son drive an old pickup to high school and college. I told him, "When you make enough money, you go buy what you want to, but right now Dad's paying for it. Here's what you're going to drive."

I learned that from my dad. He didn't have anything to give us. There's a difference between not having it to give and choosing not to give too much, though.

The kids had to work, I can tell you that. They both worked all through high school. My son worked at the Sapp Bros. operation then, and my daughter had summer jobs and babysat once in a while. They earned their own money.

It was good that they learned to make their own way financially, but even more important was that they learned to trust in God. At our house, going to church every Sunday was mandatory! Helene's family was Catholic, but as an adult she became a Protestant and a devoted churchgoer. The kids loved going to Sunday school to study the Bible stories, and we were glad to take them. Church was a place for all of us to strengthen our faith. Praying for God's guidance became a way of life for the kids, as they grew up.

God blessed me with a great son, and 99 percent of his personality he got from his mother. When Lee Alan was born, we had a big party and all the men smoked cigars. When he was little, he used to beg to go to work with me, although he was never old enough to go when I was in the food business. In fact, I didn't oblige his request until he was in high school. Then, I put him in the service department at the Ashland dealership for a while to see if he'd like it. The day he graduated from high school, he started working in the businesses with me.

Growing up, Lee Alan loved sports. He did well in all of them, and Helene and I went to every game he played in. He received an award for being the outstanding quarterback at Burke High School and then got a scholarship to go to the

University of Nebraska at Omaha (UNO) where he played the same position.

My daughter's name was Lori Ann, but we always called her Peanut, the nickname I gave her. She was always my Peanut. She was just a wonderful young lady. I still have a picture of her on my dresser from when she was a page at the Ak-Sar-Ben Ball.

You know, dads and daughters are always very close. Lori Ann and I were inseparable. She was special. We'd talk all the time on the phone if she wasn't here, and we just had a great relationship. It was the same way with my son, but I was tougher on him. Lori Ann and I were more extroverted than my son was. We were alike in our ways and in our conversation. People loved her. She was so sweet.

Lori Ann was a super athlete. During grade school, she played softball, and then in high school, she played basketball and volleyball. I helped coach all her sports, and it was wonderful to see her play. Her mom and I were so proud of her and always cheered her on from the bleachers. I tried not to miss any of her sporting events if I could help it. It was important to me to be there.

I think Lori Ann always knew she wanted to be a doctor, and her mother had a lot to do with that. Naturally, Helene, as a registered nurse herself, always encouraged her daughter to go into medicine. In fact, I believe Helene's being a nurse was one of the main reasons Lori Ann became a doctor. Ever since she was in the seventh or eighth grade, Lori Ann would say, "I'm going to be a doctor, Daddy. I'm going to be a doctor." She said that for as long as I can remember.

Lori Ann was always good in school. By the time she went to high school at Burke, she and her mother had already decided that she was going to become a doctor. Lori Ann graduated from Burke in 1980 and from Luther College in Decorah, Iowa, in 1984. When she graduated from the University of Nebraska Medical Center in 1988, with a specialty in physical medicine and rehabilitation, she became Dr. Lori Ann Sapp.

Like me and my siblings, my son and daughter were always extremely close. They were three-and-a-half years apart and always looked after one another. When Lee Alan started dating, he often took his sister along. I told him, "You'll never get married at this rate!" He always helped take care of her. When it comes to my kids, I know I'm a bit prejudiced, but Lori Ann couldn't have asked for a better brother, and Lee Alan couldn't have asked for a better sister.

There are no words to describe what a dedicated, wonderful woman my wife was. Helene was my greatest treasure. She took care of everything because I was at work all the time, from 6:00 in the morning until 9:00 at night. She took care of the kids, she mowed the yard, she picked up after me. Working as hard as she did, Helene still would find time to call me on Thursday or Friday and say, "We're going to eat by candlelight tonight," or "We're going to have lobster." She did so many things like that. I couldn't have married a nicer person. Helene could not have been more wonderful to me. She was an outstanding partner and a good Christian woman.

Women are the most unsung heroes in the world, and men don't even realize it. I mean that from the bottom of my heart. The women I have known have worked so hard for their husbands and children, cleaning up after them, cooking for them, and letting everything they do in life as wives and mothers show how much they love their family. They never rest—there's no time; they are always busy doing something for someone. Women do everything, it seems to me.

Helene and I had a lot of wonderful times with our kids. As far as I was concerned, any time with my wife, Lee Alan, and Lori Ann was a great time. Every summer, it was fun to travel to Arkansas and stay in the house we bought down there. We enjoyed being outdoors together without the pressures of work and school or keeping house. Sometimes we even invited my mom and dad to join us in our mobile home to travel around the Midwest and just be together.

Although one time we took the kids to Hawaii and had a ball, often we vacationed closer to home. When Lee Alan and Lori Ann were teenagers, I traded a truck for a lot out at Beaver Lake and built a house out there. I wasn't that good of a swimmer, but I'd take the kids around the lake and try to teach them to water-ski. Honestly, I think they probably learned more on their own, but I loved to drive the boat and watch them have fun. For a while we were going out to Beaver Lake every weekend, and the kids would have parties there sometimes. We had family reunions out there, too, come to think of it.

Lee Alan and I liked to do traditional father-son activities, like hunting and fishing, while he was growing up. Sometimes he and I would go fishing up in Canada with my friend Eugene Gottula and his son, Alan.

Quite often, I'd invite the Gottula family out to the home we had down on Beaver Lake. We'd go skiing and fishing there at the lake and just have a great time. Eugene, his wife, Ilma, and his son spent many weekends out at the lake with us. Every Sunday they were there, Helene and Ilma made delicious hand-cranked ice cream, usually vanilla, for us. Nothin' better!

Because our extended family was such a close one, we made it a priority to see each other a lot. When it was just the seven of us kids and Mom and Dad, we got together almost every weekend. But then as our own kids started growing up, we saw the rest of the family less frequently.

When I was running Snow Crop in Topeka, and Dad was short of help on the farm, I'd load up the kids and Helene on the weekend and head for Odell or wherever Mom and Dad were living at that time to help him, at least twelve hours a day. The other brothers did that, too. We were always close and always helped one another out the best we could. Family came first.

Needless to say, it was a huge party whenever we all were together. My son and daughter grew up with a big sense of family—lots of cousins and aunts and uncles. Most of the relatives they got to know were from my mother's side because Dad's people were in Illinois and Helene's family were from Pennsylvania.

Sometimes during the summer when I was in Kansas City, we'd all try to get together just for fun. We'd drive up to Nebraska with our family on a Sunday for a reunion and spend the day talking up a storm to get caught up on everyone's lives.

Other times we brothers would head to Beatrice, Nebraska, and have a reunion out there because all three sisters lived out that way. Usually, during Christmas and Easter, our family out west would come here to Omaha for the holidays. All of us—the kids, the parents, three generations of siblings, and all the in-laws—were so happy to see each other! Our times together—whenever and wherever they took place—were real blessings to us all.

The sense of family that my siblings and I grew up with was passed on to all of our children. Throughout the years, our family and our love for each other just expanded, and it was the best.

The first Sapp "coffeepot tower," at the Omaha truck stop, was originally a water tower at an Armour meatpacking plant in south Omaha. The Sapps purchased the tower and added the handle and spout. All sixteen of their travel centers feature coffeepot towers or signs, making the tower a nationally recognized symbol of the Sapp Bros.

The Sapp brothers in 1941 on their farm near Filley in southeast Nebraska. *Left to right*: Bill, Ray, Lee, and Dean.

Ray and Lee on leave from the Navy in 1947. They brought their brothers sailor hats. *Left to right*: Dean, Ray, Lee, and Bill.

The Sapp family in the late 1930s. *Seated, left to right*: Lee, Hurless, Bill, Emily, and Dean. *Standing*: Veloura, Irene, Ray, and Zelma.

Emily Sapp gives Hurless a haircut on their farm near Diller, Nebraska. The Sapps were married for fifty-two years. Emily died in 1971. Hurless passed away in 1975.

The Sapp brothers in the 1960s. *Left to right*: Bill, Ray, Lee, and Dean.

Ray and Lenora Sapp in 1963 with their four children, *left to right*: Judy, John, Jim, and Jack.

After both had lost their spouses to illness, Dean Sapp and Rose Klotz married in 1969. They're shown here in 1970 with their blended family, *left to right*: Chris, Sherilyn, Debra, Daniel, Steve, Dean, Kari, Rose, Audrey, and Claudia and her fiancé, Jack. In 1982, Daniel, 23, (inset photo) was killed in a training accident at Camp Pendleton, California.

Bill and Lucille Sapp, their four daughters, and their husbands in 2008. *Left to right:* Bob Reike, Cindy Reike, Dan Edwards, Nancy Edwards, Lucille and Bill Sapp, Suzanne Richard, Wayne Richard, Mary Ziegenbein, Kevin Ziegenbein.

Lee Sapp and Helene in 2002 with their family. *Standing*: Lee Alan, with sons, Brett and Conor, his wife, Suzanne, and his late sister, Lori Ann.

This photo from the early '90s was the last one of all the adult Sapp children together. Ray died in 1994. Dean passed away in 2003, and Veloura died in 2008. *Left to right:* Ray, Lee, Zelma, Irene, Dean, Veloura, and Bill.

The Sapps purchased the GMC truck dealership in Omaha in 1965. They sold it in 1972. *Left to right*: Ray, Lee, Bill, and Dean.

The Sapps and their wives at their Omaha GMC truck dealership in 1966. *Left to right*: Helene, Lee, Lenora, Ray, Lucille, Bill, Susie, and Dean.

The first Sapp Bros. truck stop sits on the west edge of Omaha, along Interstate 80. The Sapps purchased the land in 1966 and opened the truck stop in 1971.

Ray, Dean, Bill, and Lee at the Omaha truck stop in 1990. Sapps Bros. owns and operates sixteen truck stops between Utah and Pennsylvania. They've always credited their success to teamwork. *Photo courtesy of Omaha World Herald.*

Bill Sapp, *right*, was the catalyst behind the Roadside Chapel at the Omaha truck stop in 1976. He's shown here with Pastor L.M. Lewis. *Photo courtesy of Omaha World Herald.*

The brothers started Sapp Bros. Petroleum in 1980. The wholesale petroleum business serves all of Nebraska and parts of Kansas, Iowa, and South Dakota.

Lee and Helene Sapp accept a plaque at the dedication of the Lee and Helene Sapp Recreational Facility at the University of Nebraska at Lincoln in October 1989. The Sapps, along with their son and daughter, contributed to the University of Nebraska facility. *Photo courtesy of Omaha World Herald.*

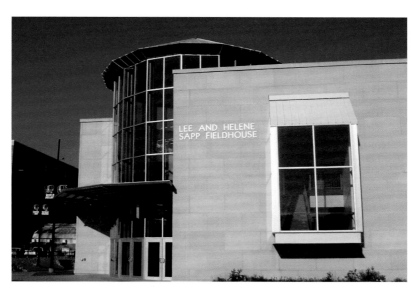

Lee Sapp was a major contributor to the University of Nebraska at Omaha for the Lee and Helene Sapp Fieldhouse, built on the campus in 1998. Lee has been a longtime supporter of athletics across the state.

HURLESS M. & EMILY V. (HUBKA) SAPP BLDG.
FILLEY RURAL FIRE STATION #1

The town fire station in Filley, Nebraska, was a gift from Lee Sapp in 1999. Built to honor his parents, the building also serves as a community center.

Lee Sapp attends a 2005 fund-raiser for the TeamMates Mentoring Program for youths in Nebraska and Iowa. *Left to right*: Warren Buffett, Nancy Osborne, Lee Sapp, Tom Osborne, and former Cornhusker Irving Fryar. *Photo courtesy of The Picture Man, Bob Olson.*

10

Pearl Rings and Curfews: Bill Sapp

Children like us who were raised in the '30s during the Depression and then went through World War II learned to make do with less stuff. We didn't have very much during those times. When the war finally ended, life changed for the better. No doubt about it, my four daughters were raised in a much different time than my wife and I were.

All of our daughters are true blessings. My first daughter, Suzanne, was the 1955 model, and we called her Suzi. She was born October 1 in Franklin, Nebraska. Then Nancy, the 1956 model, was born in November of that year. Our third daughter, Mary, came along in March of '58, and our fourth, Cindy, in July of 1960. Since I was in the car business, I related their year of birth to a car model. Within five years—from 1955 to 1960, we had four children. And all of them kept my wife, Lucille, very busy.

I have a very wonderful wife. Lucille is one of the most easygoing people I have ever met. She never gets too excited about anything. Lucille does not argue with anybody, nor does she raise her voice. My daughters told me they couldn't remember their mother ever raising her voice to them.

In our marriage, if I was making a point Lucille may have disagreed with or if I wasn't happy about something, she would just look at me. Pretty soon the tears would start. Then, I would say, "Oh, boy. You are upset, and before you get even more upset, we will end this for now." Now don't get me wrong. Lucille and I had a lot of differences in opinion, but we've never argued once in fifty-seven years, not so much because I was such a nice guy, but rather because she was such a nice lady. How do you argue with somebody who won't argue? I have been blessed with a wife who is incredibly understanding.

While the girls were growing up, I was working long, hard hours. Lucille raised the children mostly on her own. The girls really respected both of us, and we really didn't have any real problems with any of them. I think another factor that contributed to their being such fine young ladies was their Christian outlook and their accepting Jesus Christ as their Lord and Savior. And, of course, Lucille was a wonderful mother and did a terrific job.

We raised our daughters in Ashland after moving there in 1960 so I could work with Ray at the Ford dealership. They all did very well in school and were involved in many activities. Mary was the athlete. She played basketball and volleyball, but the others never really got into sports. All of my girls sang in the swing choir and each of them was a cheerleader at Ashland High School. I tried to make it to all of their games, but I didn't always succeed. Lucille would tell me, "I really think you ought to be there." I made most of them—about 97 percent of their football games and everything else. I did spend a lot of time driving my daughters and other cheerleaders to the out-of-town games.

When they were in high school, the girls had to be home by 11:00 P.M. on Friday and Saturday, and the great majority of the time, they honored their curfew. One time, however, I remember Suzi came home late on a Friday night. Usually, all of the girls would call if they weren't going to make curfew for some reason. But, Lucille and I waited and waited for Suzi to come home that night or call, but she didn't get in until quite late. The next morning, I told her, "Suzi, I am very, very disappointed in you because you didn't call, and you didn't make it home by your curfew. Your mother and I didn't want to go to sleep until we knew you were home, so we were awake a lot later than normal." Well, she told me, "Oh, Daddy, you're such a wonderful dad. The other girls' dads don't care what time they get in. I'm really sad that I disappointed you, but I'm really happy that you care."

What do you say to that?

While the kids were growing up, we took a lot of trips that I won from oil companies. I also took the family along when I went to the National Association of Truck Stop Operators (NATSO) meetings; I was on their board.

Whenever we were on vacation, it always seemed like the kids wanted to buy a lot of junk souvenirs. Lucille and I heard a lot of "Mommy, can I have this?" and "Daddy, can I have this?" I was getting tired of their wanting to buy all this junk. I said to myself, "How do you stop that?"

Well, by the time we were ready to take our family vacation to the Grand Canyon and Disneyland, I came up with a grand plan to teach my preteen and teenage daughters the value of money. It's always been my thinking that the quicker you're taught to be frugal and show good stewardship with your money, the better off you are.

Before this trip, the girls had learned they needed to work hard to earn money. Lucille and I didn't just give them anything they wanted. She and I were good examples of financial responsibility, and we didn't make purchase decisions quickly. We were never the type of parents to buy something the girls wanted just because we could afford it. Instead, we told the girls that if they wanted something, they were welcome to spend their money on it. If they needed something important, they could come to us, and we would buy it.

My wife was good at setting up things for the girls to do around the house. They received an allowance but only if they completed their assigned chores. Then, in the summertime they used to mow our lawn and the neighbors.' I furnished the lawnmower and gas, but they did all of the hard work. They'd show responsibility by doing things to earn a little money, so I would donate a bit to help them save up for special events.

On this vacation to the Grand Canyon and Disneyland, I was determined to drive home the value of the dollar. Lucille and I gave each of our children either twenty-five or fifty dollars, depending on their age. We told them, "Mom and Dad will take care of all of your expenses for food, lodging, and tickets. But, if you want any souvenirs, you need to use your money. You can spend it all the first day, or you can not spend any of it and have it all when you get back home. But it's your choice; this is your money. This is your money. Do you have any problem with that?" And the overwhelming response was, "Oh no, Daddy, that's a good deal!"

So we got into our mobile home and began our adventure. It was really a great trip because we'd travel a bit and then stay at a campground for a while. Sometimes, Mary, Cindy, and I would go out walking while Lucille, Suzi, and Nancy made the meal, although we ate out most of the time.

But one time, Mary left her purse behind on a seat at the GE Exposition. It wasn't her fault because it was so crowded. We went back to look for it, but it was gone and so she started to cry. I told her not to worry and bought her another purse and replaced her money.

116

Finally, we arrived at an attraction called Dive for Pearls. During the show, divers would go down and bring up a whole bunch of oysters. Then you could pop them open, and if you found a pearl, the divers would drill a hole in it and glue the pearl to a ring. So, I thought about it, and I told Lucille, "You know, we should have the girls do this so they can have a pearl ring. Maybe they'll keep them, and when they get older, they'll associate this family trip with their pearl ring." It seemed like a good idea to me. So I tried to talk my daughters into spending their money on the pearl rings. But all I heard from them was, "It's our money," "Oh, Daddy, we don't think we should," "We aren't going to buy that ring."

So then I bartered with them. I used my best salesmanship to try to talk them into that ring! I said, "Well, you can still have this ring years from now. When you are in high school or even married, you'll have that ring to put in your jewelry case." In the very most persuasive tone I could manage, I confided, "I really, really like that ring!" But they held their own; I couldn't convince them. It was their money. I ended up paying a portion of the cost of the rings, and they paid the rest. But, nonetheless, we got those pearl rings! And I think some of the girls still have theirs today. Interestingly, when we got home, all of them had money left over. Not one of them had spent all of her money!

That money was pretty important to them. I think that was the most important trip we ever took because, for the first time, they learned what it was like to have their own money. I think the lesson from that trip really stayed with them because all of them grew up to be very responsible with their money.

When our daughters were young, we taught them about finances. From the moment we returned from that vacation, they always took care of their own checking accounts and wrote their own checks. They could use their own money to buy things that were above and beyond what Lucille and I would buy for them.

All four of my daughters became rather conservative with their money as they grew up. In fact, when each of them turned sixteen, they came to work at the truck stop. And I paid them, of course. But before they started, I told them, "Your name is Sapp, and my name is Sapp, and this is Sapp Bros., so I expect more of you than of the other employees. If someone needs help, you need to help them. If there is a problem, you need to work it out. If you think this is too much for you, then you shouldn't work here, and I will help you get a job somewhere else." But they all said they were up for the challenge and proved to be wonderful assets to Sapp Bros.

When they went to college, I didn't give them a car. I said, "You're there at school to learn, but I will buy you a brand new car when you graduate from college." So, they all went through college, made good grades, graduated, and got jobs.

Some of the girls had part-time jobs during college; they didn't actually need one because Lucille and I were paying for most of their school costs, but they wanted to work. My daughters all worked every summer at the truck stop, and whatever they managed to save up during the summer, usually around $1,000 or so, Lucille and I would match and deposit the money into their checking account. So, by the time they graduated from the University of Nebraska at Lincoln, my alma mater, they had a pretty good-sized bank account. Even today, none of them wastes money. Not one! Eventually, they all married local boys.

To a degree, I think all of my daughters had me wrapped around their little finger. In that respect, they all took after their mother!

Part VI

Sapp Bros. Diversifies

*And we know that all things work together
for good to them that love God, to them who are
called according to his purpose.*
                              —Romans 8:28

11

From Truck Stops to Travel Centers: Bill Sapp

The good news back in 1966 was that we were selling so many GMC trucks we needed a bigger place. The bad news was that truckers were complaining that our off-the-beaten path GMC location in downtown Omaha was hard to find and difficult to get into because of the narrow streets.

Knowing all of this, we brothers discussed trying to find a location just off the interstate, so truckers could get right off and then right back on the road. When a real estate agent approached us in 1967 about land that was in a very good location right on the interstate, we were ready to listen. He said the parcel was a fifty-two-acre lot at the intersection of Interstate 80 and Highway 50 near Omaha, and we could buy at a very reasonable price.

The idea behind purchasing this land, of course, was to move the GMC dealership from Omaha and rebuild it out there. Lee and I decided that moving the GMC dealership was the thing to do, and we convinced the other brothers of it. We were all pretty aggressive thinkers, and we just felt like we didn't have room to grow and improve in downtown Omaha. So, we negotiated a deal and bought the fifty-two acres of farmland.

Soon after our purchase, however, we realized we might be in over our heads, although GMC headquarters had sent us a letter saying it was okay for us to find some land to build a larger dealership on.

We learned we would have to get commercially rezoned in Sarpy County. We didn't have any streets, water, sewers, level land—nothing. Here we were going to move our dealership from downtown all the way out there to this intersection that was not developed. We would have to build everything and pay for it ourselves, which was going to be Mission Impossible because we didn't have much cash at that point. We weren't at all sure we could come up with the kind of money we needed to build roads and get everything to operate a successful dealership.

But then a real blessing came along, although we didn't necessarily view it that way at the time. Our GMC dealership was in Douglas County, and the land we bought was in Sarpy County. There was already a GMC dealer in the small town of Papillion in Sarpy County at that time, and he told General Motors that we shouldn't be allowed to infringe on his franchise territory since this was a franchised area. That latest glitch in our plans made Dean came up with a great idea: Why not build a truck stop on the land? When we looked at the intersection and the property with that thought in mind, we could see it had tremendous potential for future development.

At that time, the fifty-mile interstate route from Lincoln to Omaha had been open to traffic for only about five years. Interstates were a relatively new concept then. America was only ten years into the whole idea of President Eisenhower's interstate highway system. In Nebraska, Interstate 80 existed only in short bits and pieces of unconnected highway in some places.

Considering history, and I like to do that, it seemed that commerce was bound to develop and grow along the interstate as it had along other transportation routes like the railroad and before that along the rivers and waterways. In 1967, Interstate 80 showed the promise of becoming one of the most traveled highways in the country, both for trucks and automobiles. Beginning in downtown San Francisco, the highway was meant to stretch all the way across the country to Teaneck, New Jersey, a suburb of New York City, with Omaha almost smack dab in the center between those two cities. That made the prospects for a truck stop look very bright. Add to that calculation the steady traffic flow on Highway 50, bringing trucks from the south into Omaha, and we had a convincing equation for business success.

Before we built anything, I grabbed a clipboard and hit the road. We did what anyone who is considering going into business should do. We researched the market, the competition, and the prospects for success.

Most of the truck stops that I knew about were making money. Both the well-managed ones and the poorly managed ones made money, but the well-managed ones made more. I went to ten truck stops to research the market. I wanted to find out the difference between a poorly managed truck stop and a well-managed truck stop.

Each time I arrived at a truck stop I looked for the person in charge and told him what I had in mind and asked if he minded answering a few questions. Most people were very cooperative, even though they knew I planned to be a competitor. That told me something right away: the operation of truck stops was a competitive business but not one that was necessarily cutthroat. I got the feeling that the other fellows that had opened truck stops were a lot like me and my brothers—people from rural areas who knew more about farms than business but wanted new challenges.

One of the people who helped me was Fred Bosselman. He owned the Bosselman Travel Center in

Grand Island. At the time I spoke to him, it was the largest truck stop between Chicago and Denver. Fred was a farmer and part-time truck driver who went on to become a legend in the truck stop field, but back then it was all pretty new to him and he was happy to answer my questions. Fred was a nice man with an honest face, and he gave me lots of important information I was able to put to good use.

Each time I did one of those interviews, I always ended the conversation by asking what he would do differently if he were to build his truck stop all over again. Everyone gave me a different answer. One person told me to be sure to put the perimeter lighting up on concrete posts; otherwise, the big rigs would knock them over, and I'd end up spending a lot of money to replace them. Another person said to have my pit designed a certain way. By the time I got back home I had a clipboard filled with ideas. I put the suggestions together and got hold of an architect by the name of Don Fry, and together we sat down and designed our first truck stop. He would eventually design most of our truck stops.

From all my research and from a business perspective, all signals were good to go for building a truck stop on our land. Our land, however, was not within the city limits, so we were pretty much on our own when it came to developing the property. We moved in thousands of yards of dirt and leveled that so that we could build. We had to put in streets and a water and sewer system. To do all that, we formed a subchapter "S" corporation and sold stock to our friends. We called the corporation B-4, which stood for the Brothers Four. Not long after that we formed the SID 48, the Sanitation Improvement District, which enabled us to sell bonds to raise money to put in the sanitation system.

We used the SID 48 to pave streets and pay for the water and sewer systems. In a business sense, we were like explorers blazing new wilderness trails. None of us had any experience doing what needed to be done. We were apprentices and CEOs at the same time.

The water tower was not planned in the beginning. I was traveling along Q Street in Omaha and a voice within told me I needed the old black Armour water tower. After checking with Paul Baburek of Plattsmouth, Nebraska, I found out that the water tower was in good shape, and we could purchase it for the price of used iron. Our water tower was not brand new, but we gave it a brand new look and that served us well over the years: the white-and-red coffeepot design eventually became a very identifiable symbol of our company. And this was God's grace.

We opened Sapp Bros. Truck Stop on June 7, 1971, even though all 455 miles of Interstate 80 in Nebraska were still three years away from completion. Because of our research and dedication to making truckers' lives better, we expected to be successful and we were.

Back then the trucker was King Kong. By that, I mean he was a powerful giant in the eyes of truck stop operators, who did everything they could think of to please him. We were no different. He was our customer and he bought lots and lots of diesel fuel, and we appreciated it.

We outfitted our building with bunk rooms upstairs and showers and a movie theater. Here's a trucker who runs his truck all day, and he doesn't get a chance to watch TV, so we put in a big screen. We'd have the movie channels and seats like you'd find in movie theaters. Back then most of the truckers were men, so we tried to provide them with those things that they wouldn't find at a motel or fast-food restaurant. They wanted comfort, but they also wanted electronic toys and pool tables, and they wanted the kind of food that men liked—steak, potatoes, apple pie, and ice cream.

When we first started, most of our store sales were truck accessories. We sold lots of mud flaps, citizen band radios, chrome lug nuts—anything and everything to do with a truck. Most of the men who drove trucks then were independent operators. They knew how to work on their trucks because they had no other choice. They couldn't call the head office and ask them to send out a repair crew.

Showers were a big attraction to truckers because they'd drive for hours on end without being able to stop long enough to clean up. They absolutely expected to have that luxury when they pulled into a truck stop. They felt they had a right to wash the road dust and diesel fuel off their arms and faces. Air-conditioned cabs didn't become commonplace until the mid-1960s. Non-air-conditioned cabs continued to be used well into the 1970s. So when I talk about road dust, I mean real grit.

We put lots of showers in that first truck stop. As time went by, we installed doors on the showers to give the truckers more privacy, but that turned out to be a bad idea because the showers were in use almost twenty-four hours a day, one right after the other. The doors wore out on a regular basis and had to be replaced.

In the early years, truckers were members of a brotherhood. Since most were owner-operators, they had a particular viewpoint on the way things ought to be done. When they turned off the motor and stepped down out of a big rig, they didn't want to be around the public. They wanted to be around people of like mind. They had their own language. They had their own dress code. And they had their own politics. They viewed truck stops as a place where they could express their individuality.

We installed telephones in the restaurant booths, so they could visit with their families or call their boss while they were eating. That way they could get back on the road as soon as possible.

Since we were open on Sundays, to accommodate truckers and travelers we decided to build a chapel and dedicate it to our parents. We had different pastors come in on Sunday morning and conduct services. My wife and I attended, and then pretty soon my brothers and their wives came and then our sisters, so it became a family affair on special occasions and provided a service for the truckers.

Later, we added a mobile chapel that was built on a trailer. We did that with a group called Transport for Christ, TFC for short. They were just starting up when we partnered with them, and today they have thirty-three locations in North America, along with active ministries in Russia and Zambia. Their ministry was based on the belief that no trucker should have to drive more than a day without being able to find a roadside chapel. We didn't put chapels—mobile or otherwise—at all our truck stops, but we did put them at locations where we thought they would be well attended.

Another action we took that made us unique was refusing to sell magazines such as *Playboy* or *Penthouse*, and we banned the sale of alcoholic beverages, including beer. Neither would we allow the sale of over-the-counter drugs that looked like uppers and downers.

We wanted our truck stops to have a family image. Everyone has seen the undercover footage on television of hookers and drugs and Lord knows what else at seedy, run-down truck stops. Whether any of that is true or not, some truck stops do have that image. We wanted no part of that, and we have worked hard to maintain a clean image. Apart from the obvious reasons for controlling our image, we discovered early on that we had a lot of non-truckers eating in our restaurants, especially families.

You might say that religion has always been is a big part of our business plan. In the early days, we began all our business meetings with prayer, and we still do today. But I don't try to force my beliefs on anyone. First, because the laws of the land are getting real strict with us about that. And, second, because I don't think you can push Jesus

Christ on any person. If you try, what usually happens is just the opposite of what you want. People become antagonistic because they don't want to be told what to believe. If they feel that pressure from you, they'll back away and won't want to have anything to do with what you have to say.

The truth is that no one can save anyone. I can encourage people to get to know Jesus Christ, but the bottom line is they have to accept Him for themselves. No one can accept the Lord for their friends. Or for their family. Or for their husband or wife. It's a personal thing. You can tell people about Him, and you can lead them to Him and say here's what He's done for me, but you can't make them believe. Sometimes I think too many people try too hard to do that.

Jesus said that you will know people by their works. So if you do the right things, and if you show love, they will know you are trying. If you feel down and out and you need help, ask Jesus to show you the way. I believe He'll give you help.

Our Omaha truck stop did so well that we decided to expand into other markets. Our second truck stop was built in Council Bluffs, Iowa. We followed the same business model that we used with the first truck stop. We scouted locations and then purchased land at busy interstate intersections or exits. In Council Bluffs, we chose acreage just off Interstate 29 at Exit 1B. We built a truck stop and a restaurant and then later added a Blue Beacon truck wash.

We were off and running at that point. I was the person who primarily oversaw the development of new truck stops. Lee and Ray and Dean were all involved in acquiring land. It was a team effort. No one person was the key to our success. It took all of us working together.

If you have a winning team, and things are working for you, people will come out of the woodwork and offer to help you. We had a lot of people help us simply because they thought we were a winning team, and they wanted to be a part of that success. We've had lots and lots of people come forward and help us by providing suggestions that we were able to use.

We bought land, sold parts of it, and developed other parts. This helped to bring the cost of land down. In the late '60s and early '70s when we were developing the land to build the truck stops, we sold lots to people who wanted to build motels, dealerships, franchises, and food operations. We continued to develop businesses as we sold land and generated capital. Capital is the lifeblood of a business. You can grow only as fast as your capital will allow you to grow. Your credit line is a valuable tool in business. We were able to buy and develop because our credit was good and, in turn, we were able to obtain more capital and build more truck stops. Another good example of doing that was our purchase of the 153-acre farm adjacent to our first truck stop property. The state and federal government wanted to put a lake on part of that land, so we sold some of it to them and watched the Corps of Engineers develop it into Wehrspann Lake. We used the money from that sale to build the Council Bluffs truck stop.

Because we stuck to our business plan, we were able to grow throughout the 1980s and 1990s and into the twenty-first century. Today we have sixteen travel centers, which we earlier called truck stops. They are listed on the next page in the order of their opening.

The Omaha travel center served as a prototype for subsequent business ventures. The Salt Lake City travel center is

- Omaha, Nebraska, 1971
- Council Bluffs, Iowa, 1978
- Fremont, Nebraska, 1982
- Cheyenne, Wyoming, 1983
- Odessa, Nebraska, 1984
- Denver, Colorado, 1986
- Columbus, Nebraska, 1987
- Peru, Illinois, 1988
- Ogallala, Nebraska, 1989
- Sidney, Nebraska, 1989
- York, Nebraska, 1989
- Salt Lake City, Utah, 1994
- Clearfield, Pennsylvania, 1996
- Lincoln, Nebraska, 1998
- Junction City, Kansas, 1999
- Nebraska City/Percival, Iowa, 2001

For more information on any of the Sapp Travel Centers, visit www.sappbrostruckstops.com

---

our biggest, not just in size—the main building has three stories compared to the two stories that most truck stops have—but in sales: almost 1.5 million gallons of diesel fuel and a quarter million gallons of gasoline are sold in a good month. Even fast food does more than one hundred thousand dollars a month.

I'd like to say that the success with that particular travel center was calculated from day one. That'd make me look like a genius. But that's not exactly the way it happened. I went to Salt Lake City with my friend and advisor Scott Brown to look at land for investment purposes, but I didn't find what I was looking for so I returned home. My brother Ray's son, Jack, and Scott's son, Ron, who was working with us at that time, located some land that they thought would be a good investment, so I flew back out there and stayed a few days to look around.

The land was in a good location, right on the Interstate 215 bypass near Interstate 80, so we put money down on an option to buy the land. But for some reason, I wasn't as sure of myself in Utah as I was in Nebraska. As a result, Scott and

130

I went to one of those companies that conduct studies on what a particular business would do in a certain location based on traffic patterns and projected growth of the surrounding community.

Without mentioning the exact location we were interested in, we told the company what we had in mind. They quoted us a price for the study, and it was considerable. We asked if they had a sample study we could see so that we would know what type of information we would get for our money. As it turned out they had just completed a Salt Lake City study, and they were happy to share it with us.

To my surprise, the study was on the exact same parcel of land I had optioned! The information they had gathered was very positive, especially when it came to traffic trends on Interstate 80. I asked Scott why they did the study. He said they did it because their customer was considering putting in a truck stop at that location. Talk about luck! I told Scott that I didn't think we would need a study, and I handed the study back to the man. He never dreamed that that location was the same location I wanted to buy. We thanked him for his time and accepted his business card and walked out the door.

Outside, we could barely contain ourselves. I knew then that I wanted that location. I found a telephone—they didn't have cell phones in those days—and I called the real estate agency and told them I wanted to exercise the option to buy. We built a larger travel center there than we had at other locations because the study we read indicated that it could handle more business than at our other locations. That turned out to be true in just about every area of sales.

When I took an option on buying that land, I had no idea that this other individual was even interested in the location. He paid for the study and I reaped the benefits. Maybe that's not fair, but it is the way things sometimes work out.

For forty years, we have gone out of our way to satisfy the needs of America's truckers. We have also looked to the future so that we can be better prepared for changes in the market. You have to do that in business. You can't sit still and ignore market trends and expect continued profits.

A book that came out in 1998, *Who Moved My Cheese?* by Spencer Johnson, points out that as life goes by, the cheese moves and you have to move with the cheese or go hungry. Years ago, when they came out with the first car, the harness manufacturer or the carriage manufacturer probably said something like, "Well, that thing will never go." And they kept right on building their carriages and harnesses. It was a long period of time, maybe ten years, before the sale of automobiles started to overtake carriages. By then, it was too late for carriage and harness makers to adjust to the changing times. It's that way with most anything.

Today's businesses change even more quickly, partly because of new government regulations that seem to multiply each year and partly because of the widespread use of computers that provide business owners with more and more information about their sales and their potential market. Trucks now even have satellite domes on them so they can communicate more easily with the home office and be quickly located by it.

When we first started, we did everything to please the trucker. About 80 percent of our diesel fuel customers were owner-operators and 20 percent were fleets. Today, however, those numbers are probably reversed.

One of the things that helped me stay on top of the trends was my membership in the National Association of Truck Stop Operators. I represented Nebraska through the years and served on many boards. We'd have two conventions a year, and all the sellers would set up booths to display what they had in the way of new merchandise. I'd go there and learn about new equipment and new pumps.

We learned a lot from the association about what the truckers wanted. We also were able to form relationships with manufacturers so we could buy directly from them. That type of arrangement worked out well, especially with tires. For years we bought tires from Goodyear, but then we were able to reach agreements with overseas manufacturers to buy direct from them, cutting out the middleman and his profits. Today we have some of the best prices in the country for tires.

In business, change can be your friend, but only if you prepare yourself for its arrival. I think in the years to come, our travel center business will change greatly. I foresee the day when customers will pull into a travel center and eat dinner while their electric car is plugged into a charger that we will provide for, say, a five-dollar fee. They'll finish eating and go out and unplug their car and head on down the road. I imagine the new electric cars will have motors that will charge the batteries while the engine is running, but that probably will not be enough to keep the batteries fully charged. If you are on the road and you're going a long distance, you will have to charge it somewhere.

Regardless of what happens in the years ahead with electric cars, interstate travelers are going to need showers and food. Today we have showers for men and women and the showers are different from the ones we had in the early years. We are seeing more and more lady truckers—and, yes, female truckers can be ladies—so we are changing our facilities to accommodate both sexes.

These days our showers are built for privacy without the need for doors or curtains. The walls are all tile and the showers are designed for the water to spray onto the tile walls so that when you need to clean the showers you just wipe down the walls. Men and women appreciate clean facilities and we have housekeepers going into the showers every hour to make certain that everything is super clean.

I'm sure our restaurants will change with the times as well and provide a more pleasant dining experience by offering more healthful food and a larger selection of vegetables and fruits. The public knows what it wants, and if you don't listen, you can't expect to continue to make a profit.

You can travel the interstates of this country from coast to coast and find truck stops that are on their last legs. They look run-down and badly in need of paint. Service is almost non-existent. At one time those truck stops were brand new and had a great future ahead of them. They started slipping the day the ownership stopped investing in the future. We don't intend to join that crowd.

Whatever the future holds for us, if we welcome change, I am confident that we will continue to have good travel centers.

12

Sapp Bros. Petroleum: Bill Sapp

By 1980, our truck stops were doing quite well, and we were buying large quantities of diesel fuel and gasoline, then selling it for an acceptable profit. The more diesel and gasoline we bought, the better prices we were able to get in some cases. With better buying power, we were able to sell wholesale to volume customers.

Finally, we reached a point when we had to have someone oversee the wholesale business. Bernie Raiter, who had worked as third shift manager of the truck stop in Omaha, was given the job and a desk there. He shared office space with Keith Swearingen, the manager who ran our service bays at the truck stop.

In the beginning, our wholesale business didn't have a name. The operation was simply another division of our truck stop business. All that began changing when Bernie started calling on customers. Whenever we got a good price on fuel for our retail operations, Bernie called up potential customers—truck lines, construction companies, and electrical companies, to name a few—to offer them a good deal on fuel. When you get down to it, there aren't many business people who will turn down a good deal—and not many of them said "no" to Bernie, especially when he started telling them right off that he had a deal for them.

Soon after Bernie started working the accounts, we realized we had something worth developing. We spun off a separate business, created a corporation, and named it Sapp Bros. Petroleum. We started with a truck and a trailer to serve clients in Omaha, and then, as time went by, we added more truck stops and continued growing the wholesale business, as well.

For example, we put smaller motors and economical transmissions in our trucks because we had no plans to run them in the mountains where we'd need extra power. On top of that, we have always taken very good care of our trucks. In addition, getting the right equipment for the right job is very important. It's important to do research before you buy equipment.

To be successful in business, you have to have the mental flexibility to be able to adjust to changing conditions. One day Bernie said we needed some new trucks. On the face of it, it was a reasonable request. But why would we do that? We had trucks that we ran ten hours a day and then sat parked for fourteen hours. Instead of getting new trucks, we needed to drive the trucks we had day and night. When we started doing that, it worked out well because a lot of our customers were city dealers who closed at night. We serviced them during the day and then transported fuel to our truck stops at night. Truthfully, you can run your trucks at night and get more loads hauled more efficiently because in the daytime you have to put up with heavy traffic and waiting in line at the pipeline.

Every truck is analyzed for profit and, therefore, we know what every truck makes us or doesn't make us. One thing we discovered that works well for us is paying bonuses to drivers who work at night. As far as I know, no one else was doing that when we started. Sometimes to make money you have to spend money. Bonuses for drivers to work at night translate into greater profits for the company.

Some people view us as trendsetters, but it is not because we entered the business with a lot of experience. I came into the business pretty much as a stranger. I didn't come into the business because my father was a jobber and taught me everything that he knew about driving trucks. I didn't come into it because he'd run a service station or a truck stop. I came into the business with experience as a farm boy, teacher, and salesman. I think that helped me to see the business with more clarity than someone who had been brought up around trucks or gas stations. I took nothing for granted. I challenged old ways of doing things.

When we first started, most jobbers drove tank wagons that held between 1,500 and 2,500 gallons of fuel. Most of the trucks we put in had a 4,750-gallon capacity; consequently, one driver could deliver almost twice as much in a day, making that unit much more efficient.

We own bulk tanks where we store fuel, but, whenever possible, we transport directly from the pipeline terminal to the consumer. Every time you handle fuel, you lose one-fourth of 1 percent on average, so if you handle it four times, you lose 1 percent or a gallon out of a hundred gallons. We have been able to sell 100 percent of what we buy because we buy it at the pipeline and minimize the number of times that we handle it before it is delivered to the consumer. That way we lose no measurable amount of fuel. We also save inventory costs since we do not have to store the fuel before it is delivered.

13

Sapp Bros. Propane: Bill Sapp

S uccess breeds success. If you get a taste of it, you naturally want more. Nothing wrong with that. That's the way the Lord made us.

Sapp Bros. went through a process like that with our truck stops. When they proved to be a successful investment, we were motivated to branch out into the petroleum industry and start selling gasoline and diesel. Once that paid off for us, we investigated the potential for selling propane gas.

We were familiar with propane because we used it to heat our buildings. Natural gas was not available at our location since it is expensive for natural gas companies to put down pipes to deliver it in sparsely populated areas. We purchased propane and stored it in thirty-thousand-gallon tanks and then piped it into our building.

The main difference between propane and natural gas is that natural gas comes from the ground and propane is a by-product of both the crude-oil refining process and natural gas processing. Another difference is that natural gas is lighter than air and propane gas is heavier than air. Propane is delivered to the customer in a truck and pumped into a steel tank—usually small and round but invariably painted white. The propane is then piped into a house or business where it is used for heating and cooking purposes.

There are entire communities in Nebraska that can't get natural gas. When you drive through those little towns you notice those little white tanks in the backyards, house after house. Of course, we weren't thinking about all that when we began. We were focused on taking care of our own needs. We used enough propane that we figured out that we could probably get discounts if we purchased directly from the source. One thing led to another and we made a deal with Phillips 66 so that we could become a distributor and purchase the propane wholesale.

Propane is odorless and colorless in its natural state. For that reason a commercial odorant is added so that its smell can be detected if it leaks. Most people are surprised to learn that propane is an approved, alternative clean fuel listed in the 1990 Clean Air Act.

As time went by, we used the same game plan we used with our truck stop and petroleum divisions. We increased profits by expanding operations. Rather than go into new markets to compete with existing propane companies, we purchased or merged with those companies, including:

- Allen Oil
  Irvington, Nebraska

- Poland Oil
  Grand Island, Nebraska

- Pro Oil
  Ogallala, Nebraska

- Lohr Petroleum
  Columbus, Nebraska

- Nielsen Oil and Propane
  West Point, Nebraska

- Dettleson Oil
  North Platte, Nebraska

- Oil Products Company
  Omaha, Nebraska

- Fuel Tech
  Blair, Oshkosh, and North Platte, Nebraska

- Ferrell Gas
  Butte, Nebraska

- Salem Oil Co.
  Lincoln, Nebraska

- Wemart
  Barlett, Nebraska

- Jurgens
  Filley, Nebraska

- Wymore Oil
  Wymore, Nebraska

- Pollard Oil
  Clarks and Fullerton,
  Nebraska

- Smith Oil
  Salix, Iowa

- TriState
  Sioux City, Iowa

- James Bros.
  Falls City, Nebraska

- Ward Propane
  Elgin, Nebraska

- Naper Gas
  Naper, Nebraska

- Beck Oil
  Decatur, Nebraska

Today Sapp Bros. is the largest propane distributor in the state of Nebraska. I don't want any glory, though, for the success of Sapp Bros. Petroleum and Propane, although I'm proud of the work we have done and continue to do. The businesses have succeeded only because I've had the help and advice of a lot of good people along the way. It was because of people like Bernie Raiter, Allen Marsh, John Hoffert, Don Quinn, and the folks who worked with them that we were able to grow and keep growing, and I am grateful to them.

Part VII

Ties That Bind

To every thing there is a season,
and a time to every purpose under the heaven:
A time to be born, and a time to die; a time to plant,
and a time to pluck up that which is planted…
                            —Ecclesiastes 3:1, 2

14

Family First: Lee Sapp

As the years went on, knowing our parents were proud of us and of our accomplishments meant a great deal to all of us brothers. With each success of ours, they about bust their buttons. One of the best things about making a few dollars over the years was the opportunity it gave us to help Mother and Dad have a better life.

When I was still in the food business working for Snow Crop, I happened to be down at the University of Texas and noticed a very busy car wash right across the street from the campus. All of a sudden, I had a great idea I couldn't wait to share with my brothers! When I got back, I suggested we move the folks off the farm because they still were having a hard time, buy them a house in Lincoln, and build a car wash next to the university so Dad could run it. They agreed it was a pretty good idea and would solve some problems for everyone. It did—in fact, that was probably the best living our mother and dad ever had.

While our parents were living in the house the brothers bought them, four college kids rented the basement. Mother really seemed to enjoy them. She didn't have to feed them, but Dad would invite them up to supper all the time. Mother would always make them say a prayer before they all ate. My mother was a big-hearted lady and was always helping people. She was always that way. Mother just loved to help people and she was that way 'til the day she died of a stroke in 1971.

Besides having great parents, I have been blessed with three wonderful older sisters, and I've never forgotten all they have given me throughout my life. All of us brothers had great relationships with our sisters. When we were young and we got out of hand, our sisters put us in our place. Later on, when they got their cars, we brothers changed their oil and serviced their cars for them. We all tried to help each other whenever we could. There was great love there.

My oldest sister, Irene, was a very generous, caring person. And pretty! She was even Miss Beatrice in the 1939 Miss Nebraska pageant. Later on, Irene married a wonderful man named Guy Brubaker. He was an insurance man from Holmesville, Nebraska. Irene and her husband moved to Colorado and were out of the area, so we didn't see much of her. Irene lives in a nursing home in Beatrice now.

My second sister, Veloura, became a schoolteacher and married Glen Barnard—a farmer and one fine man. And boy, was he a workaholic. He was up by five o'clock every morning. I went over and worked for him sometimes. He taught all of us brothers how to work. Glen was a wonderful husband to Veloura. She passed away February 27, 2008.

Now, my sister Zelma was the youngest of the three sisters. Both Zelma and Veloura attended Peru State College, just like our mother. In fact, both Zelma and Veloura bore a striking resemblance to our mother in many ways. They were pretty near the spittin' image of her. And when you'd go to either one of their houses, you wouldn't leave there without something to take home with you—anything from a cracker with butter or peanut butter on it to an entire pie.

Most of us have that same habit, actually. Zelma, like our mother, could make a heck of a kolache. She is eighty-six years old now and lives with her husband, Kenny, in Beatrice. She's still got a great attitude and positive outlook on life. Zelma wrote a poem called "Gifts from Mother," and it means a lot to all of us.

Gifts from Mother
To Emily's Children

What was the most special gift our mother gave you?
Was it discipline or the love of learning she taught us
    to pursue?
Was it her generosity or her courage and faith she showed
    to us each day?
Or was it the love she gave to each of us
    in her special way?
For me, it was her examples of guidance
    with the demands of our family in tow;
How she cared so gracefully for all her seven children,
    I'll never know.
Each of us had problems that made us need her most;
She provided food and the extras for all of us—
Amazing how she could stretch a roast!
Mother could draw flowers and farm animals
    very life-like to see;
Through her talent and understanding of life,
    she taught us how to be.
Mother had advice for the four brothers
    who would wrestle each other all day
But when outsiders came to fight, would stick together
    like bales of hay.
I remember Mother saying—"If you have one stick,
    it can bend and break in two,
But four sticks are strong, so together show the world
    what you brothers can do."

Mother faced fears and disappointments
  we have not known;
But, thankfully, she lived to see all her children grown
  and in happy homes.
Mother taught us how to live, helping us handle
  our problems and strife.
Because of her, we know what things are most important,
  and we thank God for these gifts of life.

All of my sisters, including Veloura when she was alive, have been wonderful, caring people, and all three of my brothers-in-law are fantastic, as well. They have taken good care of their wives and have been so kind to us brothers.

Every third or fourth Sunday, I try to get to Beatrice to visit Irene and Zelma and their husbands. I go to see Irene at the nursing home in the morning and then attend church with Zelma and Kenny. After church, Guy joins us for lunch at Zelma's, and we have a great time talking. Doing what it takes to keep family close is very important to me and I enjoy it.

My wife, Helene, enjoyed life, too. She was giving and caring and loved by a lot of people—she was just an incredible woman. Helene came from the coal mines of Pennsylvania, and, like us, she grew up without a lot of advantages. Her parents had ten girls and one boy, and she was in the middle. Some of the children died during infancy; I think the boy may have been one of them. I believe three of the eleven did not survive childhood. Helene's family was poor. Her dad died pretty young of black lung disease when Helene was just eight or nine years old. She hardly remembered her father, actually.

I am not sure how her mother managed to make a living and support all of those kids after her husband passed away. As soon as those kids got out of school, they all went their separate ways, but they supported their mother until she passed at age sixty-seven, shortly before we got married. Helene had to work her way through nursing school to become an ensign in the Navy.

Actually, I didn't know Helene's background until I went back to Pennsylvania to visit her family with her. I think the fact that Helene and I had a similar upbringing made us a good match. We both learned that the harder you work, the further you get, and we both valued God, integrity, honesty, and conservatism.

By the time Helene and I married, she had only seven living siblings, and I got to know them very well. We had a sister of hers from California as a bridesmaid at our wedding, but we didn't travel to California to visit her two sisters who lived there or back to Pennsylvania for four or five years after we were married. I believe that another sister passed during that time. Helene's sisters visited us here in Nebraska and stayed with us sometimes, and then we would go back and stay with them in Pennsylvania. We had a lot of good times. She came from a good family with good people. But Helene was the only one out of the whole bunch who lived in the Midwest.

Even though Helene has passed away now, her family still calls me and travels to Omaha to see me. In fact, her sister Eva's kids were here recently, and I got a beautiful card from them thanking me for the hospitality. I am still very close to Helene's family.

Helene sure did admire my mother. I think I would have really liked her parents, too, but they were both gone before we got married, so I never got to know them. Because none of Helene's sisters lived near us, our kids didn't get to know any of them too well. Our kids got to visit with their aunts on their mom's side a bit, though, when they came to visit. They would stay for a few days or a week at a time, but then the kids wouldn't see them again for another two or three years.

I am a very lucky man. Helene loved me and the kids, and I loved her for fifty-four years and five months. We had a wonderful life together. I was blessed all the way around. Helene and I were like two big kids, the way we enjoyed our life together.

The great thing was that Helene loved me in spite of my faults. I am quite set in my ways, no doubt about it. She joked with me a few times about that. She'd say, "Did anybody ever call you a hard-headed Sapp?" And I'd say, "Yeah, several."

Helene and I were not the only happy couple in our family, though. The Sapp family is full of strong marriages, actually. No Sapp ever did get a divorce.

Helene and I felt so good about our kids. We tried to teach them both our favorite four letter word—W-O-R-K.

Lee Alan is a wonderful son. He's been working at the Ashland dealership for thirty years now. He always wanted to be a car dealer, see. Brother Bill and I have both tried to talk to him about his career to see if he might want to join Sapp Bros. Petroleum or do anything else, but he is happy as a hog in slop out there running that dealership! Lee Alan is in love with the car business.

In 1960, we four brothers bought the Ford dealership in Ashland. We kept it for six years, and then we moved to Blair. Ron Grebe and his partner bought it from us in 1966. Well then in 1977, my son and I bought Ron Grebe out and got it back, and Lee Alan has been there ever since.

Ron Grebe is a wonderful man and is still a very good personal friend of mine. He's retired in Lincoln now, but he still sells cars for us out of Ashland occasionally. He had a great following throughout the years at the dealership. The three of us—Ron, Lee Alan, and me—had a great relationship, professionally and personally. I will be forever indebted to Ron.

Lee Alan and I ran the dealership together in Ashland for many years. Sometimes he would say, "Hey, Dad, I have an idea…." And then I would say, "Well, tell me what you want to do and how you would do it?" That would put him right back into the soup. And then if it was a good enough idea, I would let him do it any way he wanted. I thought he could learn a lot by doing things himself. What I always focused on, besides the employees, was the profit and percentage of profit. I would say, "If you do this, you may not have anything down here at the bottom line."

The Ashland dealership is Lee Alan's place now. He's a workaholic and has done a fabulous job with the dealership. He gets to work every day at 6:30 or 7:00 A.M., and I talk to him nearly every morning around 7:00. When we're ready to say good-bye, I still say "I love you," and he still says, "I love you." We have a very close relationship.

Lee Alan and his Uncle Bill are a whole lot alike. They are both very strong Christians. During the week, Lee Alan gets up early to make it to Christian meetings with ministers and other Christian men. He and Bill get people together and bring them over to God's side, and they do a great job of it. Bill thinks the world of him and always tells me what a great son I have.

Lee Alan also is a tremendous leader in the community and knows a lot of people. Many times, people from Gretna and Ashland have sent their kids who've gotten in trouble to see my son for help. Lee Alan is as close to Tom Osborne, the former football coach at Nebraska and now the athletic director, as any man I've known. I am very, very proud of Lee Alan. Of course, I give 99 percent of the credit to his mother. I am such a lucky man.

My daughter, Lori Ann, was a really good Christian, as well. She became a doctor and was in charge of a section of a hospital in Des Moines. She had always wanted to be a doctor, and she was a natural. Lori Ann definitely chose the right field. She loved helping people. She had a lot of her mother in her like that. It's really something that both Lori Ann and her brother, Lee Alan, took after their parents so much—Lori Ann being in the medical profession like her mother, and Lee Alan going into business with me.

My son and daughter were always very close. Even as adults, they talked all the time. They both had gone to the Presbyterian church down the road every Sunday while they were growing up and became models of integrity, in my eyes. After they moved out of the family home, they would each carry the Bible with them so they could go through it together when they talked on the phone. That's just something they started doing on their own in 1985 after they graduated from high school; we didn't suggest it or anything.

After high school, Lori Ann was away from home studying to be a doctor, and Lee Alan had graduated from college. They would have been young adults when they started staying in touch regularly and talking about spiritual things, like their walk with the Lord Jesus. Lori Ann and Lee Alan would talk on the phone on Sunday mornings when she was out of town, but they kept it up even after she moved back to Omaha. And this went on until she passed away. They would even take vacations together sometimes. They went down to Arizona to the Grand Canyon for five days once with some other people around their age. Lee Alan and Lori Ann had a very special relationship—I haven't seen anything like it in any other family I've known.

Brother Ray and Brother Dean were both good family men, as well. The brothers were excellent fathers to their children, and their family always came first.

Helene and I had some good friends that we considered our extended family. Eugene Gottula and his wife,

Ilma, were certainly part of that group. As I mentioned earlier, I met Eugene when we were very young—just five years old. His dad was a farmer, just like mine. For some reason, Eugene and I really hit it off. His cousin was Don Bartels, our neighbor, so I got to know both of the boys real well.

Gene always lived down in Elk Creek, Nebraska, and we used to go fishing and hunting down there together. Gene was quite the hunter and the fisherman. We'd stay at each other's houses sometimes and even flew overseas together with our wives. Our families spent a lot of time together, and our sons grew up enjoying each other's company, just as Gene and I had done. We always got along real well and just loved spending time together. When Eugene passed away in 2006, we had been friends for a very long time—nearly sixty years.

Back in the early years, when Helene was sick with tuberculosis in the hospital at Excelsior Springs, I'd visit her twice a day. Little did we know that when she recovered, we would be off traveling the world.

Our trip to China was a memorable one. It was the Richard Nixon era, and Helene and I were two of about three hundred Americans invited to visit that country. I think Alan Beerman, the Nebraska Secretary of State at the time, had everything to do with our being chosen to visit China. See, I had taken several business trips with him before, and he was a good friend of mine. Alan was just an old farm boy at heart. We went to Czechoslovakia with Alan, too. In fact, he'd ask us on pretty near every trip he would take. About China, all I know is that Helene and I received a letter from President Nixon inviting us to go. He was eager to see relations between the two countries improve and thought having businessmen and their wives visit would help speed the process. We also got a letter from President Nixon thanking us for going after we returned to the United States.

Helene and I had a wonderful life, no doubt about it. She took excellent care of me, our children, and our home. After the children left the nest, Helene decided to return to nursing and worked at Veteran's Hospital for ten or twelve years. She'd occasionally visit the bank I owned in Ashland and eventually decided she'd like to work there. I was concerned with her decision because, at that point, I could tell she was starting to forget things and wasn't acting quite normal. Soon I believed Helene was starting to show symptoms of Alzheimer's, so, in 1996, I drove her up to the Mayo Clinic. That's when she received the actual diagnosis.

Several years later, Helene was getting sicker and sicker. She just kept going downhill, as Alzheimer's patients do. By 2004, Helene could not function on her own, and we reached a point where we were going to have to put her in a nursing home. As Helene's condition worsened, my daughter came home more and more frequently. One day Lori Ann came to me and said, "Dad, I'm quitting the hospital to come home and take care of Mother."

So Lori Ann did just that. She quit her job at the hospital in Des Moines and moved back here to take care of her mother. Lori Ann had worked hard to become a doctor, and she was really enjoying practicing medicine at the time that her mother got sick. But Lori Ann gave all of that up to move back to Omaha and care for her mother full-time. That's the kind of person she was. She'd come over at six o'clock in the morning and care for her mother all day. Then I'd get home at 4:30 or five o'clock and let her go home. And she kept that schedule up for a little over a year. And then, our family was dealt a horrible blow.

In the late summer of 2004, Lori Ann, went on a sixteen-mile bicycle ride. When she came home, she said she

152

was feeling very weak. I remember saying to her that a sixteen-mile bike ride was enough to make any person weak. But since she was a doctor, she had a sense that something else might be wrong.

She went to a doctor, and at first he thought she had pneumonia. She was given antibiotics. But, she kept getting sicker, and it turned out she had non-Hodgkins lymphoma, which is a cancer of the body's lymph system. By the time the doctors realized the problem, complications had set in and she was gone in two weeks. She passed away on September 23, 2004. My daughter was only forty-two years old.

After Lori Ann passed away, I had to put Helene in a nursing home. I was there for breakfast and supper—at least twice a day—but she didn't know me. She didn't know me; she didn't know the grandkids; she didn't know anybody. The kids would show her pictures of me, but she had no idea who I was. She spoke very little in the end. As soon as I'd get there, though, she would want to hold my hand.

After living about two or three years in the nursing home, Helene passed away in 2008. She had battled Alzheimer's for twelve years. That disease changes people's worlds. It changed Helene's, and it changed everyone's world who loved her.

I have a wonderful relationship with my grandchildren. Lee Alan is raising his children much in the same way that Helene and I raised him and his sister. My two grandsons—Brett and Conor—and I have done just about everything together. I've gone on trips with them, and I golf with them now that they are big enough.

I really enjoy spending time with the boys. Before the oldest one, Brett, went off to college, we used to do even more together than we do now. Every Friday night last fall, I went to my younger grandson's football games in Ashland

and watched him play. Almost every Sunday, Lee Alan, Suzanne, and Conor come see me, and we eat together.

My grandson Brett is twenty-one now and is on an academic scholarship down at Washington College, a very well-known college in St. Louis. Brett is doing great at Washington College; his grades are excellent. He is also involved in sports. The last two years, the basketball team Brett has played on has taken the National Championship in Division III.

Brett is considering studying to be either an engineer or a doctor. I asked him why the medical field and he said, "Well, I just think a person makes a lot of money doing that." I told him, "Maybe so, but are you going to be happy there?" It's really too early to know what career he will choose eventually. A lot of people his age change their minds.

My other grandson, Conor, is seventeen now and looks like a Sapp with a beard. He's an Ashland High School football player and a force to be reckoned with. At six foot one and 185 pounds, he is fast. He plays quarterback on offense and alternates playing the position with another guy. In fact, he plays both offense and defense and has even run the football back sixty-one yards for a touchdown. Of course, it's just a grandpa's opinion, but I think he's their best varsity player so far. I hope Conor will go to college here in Nebraska on a scholarship, if he is good enough. If he isn't good enough, he doesn't deserve it. We are Nebraska people, and if he would ever be good enough to play football at Nebraska in Lincoln or Omaha, that would be great.

Both of my grandsons are full of spunk. I guess we all were at that age. The world hasn't changed that much. It won't be long now until they will be going with girls, getting married, and having kids of their own someday. I would be a great-grandpa then. I hope I live that long. I am one lucky man.

15

Generations: Bill Sapp

We brothers always knew the time would come when Dad couldn't farm anymore. That time came in 1960 when I was selling insurance for Prudential.

When we heard of Dad's decision to quit farming, Lucille and I invited him and Mother to move to Lincoln and live in the duplex next door to our house. We brothers had just bought it as an investment and thought it would be perfect for them. We got that nice two-story house all fixed up, and Mother and Dad took us up on our offer and moved in. It felt good to have them close and know that I was right there if they needed anything. We rented out their basement to four college students, so it was a full house. Those college students really loved Mother and Dad. Mom would make a pie or a cake and take it down there to them all the time.

As soon as we were financially able, all four of us brothers wanted to make our parents' lives easier. We all recognized that most of our personal and professional success was built on lessons learned at home during our growing-up years. And we loved our parents dearly for making all the sacrifices they made for us through the years.

After Mother and Dad moved into the house next door to me, Lee and Dean turned one of the blocks across from the stadium into a car wash and a parking lot. Dad helped run both of them. During football season, he really seemed to get into the crazy spirit of Game Day at Nebraska as he parked the cars in the lot.

I have to say that, surprisingly, we made a lot more money on the parking lot than we did on the car wash. We got five dollars per car and could get fifty or sixty cars in there at once on Game Day. People would park their cars and just walk right across the street to the football game. We'd sit there in the parking lot with our radio on listening to the game. A win-win situation! We made more money on car parking in one night than we did the whole month on washing them!

Dad helped with the car wash, too. People would give him quarters and dimes for the car washing service back when they made those coins out of real silver. Mother saved the dimes and quarters from the car wash days and gave them to her children, even though we were all adults by then.

Our mother was a very good woman. She was always so hardworking and well organized. Mom was also a good planner, a good cook, and the leader in our home growing up. You know, when you go to a couple's house, one is usually more in charge. Mother was very loving but could take charge when she needed to. When Dad didn't fill the bill, Mom stepped up, but when Dad was the leader, she'd step down.

I remember one day Dad called me and said that he thought that Mother's iron had fallen and hit her on the head. What had actually happened was that she had a cerebral hemorrhage and a blood vessel broke; she had had a stroke. I just prayed to the Lord then. We took her to the hospital and called all of the brothers and sisters to come up right away to see her. She went downhill real quickly, though. Mother passed away the same day.

Mom died in 1971, the year we started the truck stop. Fortunately, she lived long enough to see all of us succeed. We all made it. The brothers and I had been in the car business for eleven years by that time. A lot of us kids did well in business, and we all succeeded in our relationships. Not one of us divorced our spouses, and I think Mom was happy about that.

Dad lived four more years after Mother passed. After Mom was gone, Dad stayed in the same house they lived in for a while, but it became difficult for him to manage on his own. I remember telling him he could come live with us if he wanted to. But Dean and Ray were all living in Blair at the time, and there was an assisted-living home there, so we thought that might be the best place for him.

Dad did very well there for about eighteen months, residing in the independent-living area of the facility. He always wore a sports coat and a tie, and he played pool and even had a car of his own for a while. He called the Methodist pastor who was the head of the place "The Boss" and enjoyed talking with him.

Dad passed away in 1975 of diabetes complications. He was seventy-nine years old, and I think that was a blessing that he passed on quickly. He had lived a full life and raised his children well, with the help of my mother, of course. I think it's a blessing for parents to see their children turn out all right. The Lord was good to my parents and took them when it was their time.

Although there's no such thing as the perfect marriage, I believe I've had the greatest marriage anyone possibly could have. My wife, Lucille, was a farm girl. Her dad had a huge farm, and she was raised very conservatively. To this day, she is very frugal with money. If I try to buy her something expensive, more often than not, she'll say, "I don't want it and I won't wear it. I feel uncomfortable in it, so don't buy it, please!"

But she does know what she wants. One time, I was trying to figure out something to buy her for her birthday. All she kept telling me was that she wanted a new front storm door. She thought she needed it because one time when our daughter Suzi was staying with us, as she liked to do sometimes, her dog opened the nice glass storm door at the front of the house a few times and left some scratch marks on it.

Lucille had told me that she wanted it fixed, so I went out there and looked at it. I had to say to her, "Lucille, I'm telling you, there isn't one person out of a hundred that could see those marks." See, you had to get down and really look hard to see the scratches. I could see some when the light shined just right on it, but they were insignificant. The door was still a good door. But she kept on saying, "I just think we need a door that doesn't have any scratches on it."

By her birthday, I had already picked out a very nice card from Hallmark, but I was still thinking hard about what I could buy her that she would like. She opened the card and said, "Oh, thank you!" And then at that moment, I thought of the perfect present. I told her, "The gift this year will be a new storm door!" She said, "Well, how quickly can you get it?" And I said, "We can get it today." So we went up there to the store, and she spent about an hour picking it out. She chose a green-and-blue-panel storm door. Then, we went home and our neighbors came over and helped us put it up. And Lucille was really, really happy about this storm door. That was her idea of a great birthday present!

While our four daughters were growing up, we liked to do a lot of traveling. Every year we would take a big trip and we would take everybody with us—even the boyfriends or husbands of our daughters. We took those girls all over the United States; in fact, we still take them everywhere. We've also taken them, as adults, to Florida, Hawaii, and the Bahamas. Even after they were all married, Lucille and I took all of them on an Alaskan cruise. In fact, last year, our entire family flew down to Phoenix to a home we own down there. Our family has taken a great many trips throughout the years.

Our girls are all grown up now, and all of them are married. Three of them live in the Omaha area. Suzanne and her husband, Wayne Richard, live in a very nice home in Naperville, near Chicago. Wayne was a local boy from Ashland whose dad ran the co-op station. He and Suzi dated a little in high school, although she was a grade ahead of him. Then they went to college. Suzi was a hard worker and majored in home economics. They waited for him to graduate, and then they got married. They moved around a few times, but they finally settled in Chicago with Wayne working at the Board of Trade. Wayne has done very well. Suzi works independently as an interior decorator.

Then our daughter, Nancy, married Dan Edwards. Dan's father, Dick Edwards, worked for the Farmers and Merchants National Bank. They had gone to high school and college together and were in the same class. Dan came to me one day after he'd graduated from college and asked, "Can I marry your daughter?" Of course, I said "yes." They got married and then moved to St. Louis so Dan could work for a hospital. Nancy had excellent business sense and a very good job working for Neiman Marcus. Then they moved back up here, and Dan went into business for himself. He has a convenience store and runs it now. Nancy works with him in the business.

My daughter Mary, on the other hand, is married to a very successful farmer named Kevin Zigenbein. He's a local boy, too, and farms about three thousand acres near

159

Ashland. Mary didn't know him during high school, but he went to school just a few miles away in Mead, Nebraska. Their farm was just seven miles out of Ashland. They met on a blind date. Mary taught for a number of years after they married. She was a physical education teacher at Elkhorn Junior High School and was even named Teacher of the Year once. She really enjoys coaching girls' volleyball and still coaches part-time at the school as well as runs a gift store in Ashland. I don't know how she finds the time to do all that and still be an active community worker, a church worker, and the mother of three. She just does everything.

Our youngest daughter, Cindy, married Bob Rieke, an Omaha attorney, a partner at one of the largest law firms in Omaha. Cindy went into business as a buyer at Richman-Gordman and didn't marry Bob until she was thirty-five.

For the longest time, Cindy and Bob had two dogs and one cat but no kids. They wanted them, but it just wasn't happening for them. Cindy's sisters started giving them gifts for their pets because Bob and Cindy didn't have any children. But then, Cindy and Bob adopted a baby boy, and everything changed. They named him Max. All of a sudden, the cat ran away because she didn't get any attention anymore, and one of the dogs became the guardian of that little baby. He was a six-month-old preemie and had a lot of health problems, but he's healthy now. Bob and Cindy are so devoted to him, you can't believe it. Before Max came along, Cindy worked and made good money, and Bob also made a lot of money. But it wasn't enough. Max just really changed their lives more than anything else.

My brother Lee had two wonderful children. I never had a son of my own—I had four wonderful girls—but Lee's son, Lee Alan, stands out to me among all of the boys in the family. Lee Alan is a fine athlete, a good citizen, a terrific nephew, and an ideal son. He is honorable and respectful to his father and is committed to the Lord. He also runs that dealership in a good fashion and is a very hard worker. He gets up early and works long hours. If I were going to raise a son, and he turned out anything like Lee Alan, you can believe I would feel blessed.

And Lee's daughter, Lori Ann, was so loving. She sold her share of her medical practice in Des Moines to come back and commit the rest of her life to taking care of her mother. I think when she moved back to Omaha she was concerned that her mother was not going to live much longer. She came home and bought her house in Tiburon, which wasn't too far from her mother's house. Lori Ann would take her mom different places, visiting Lee Alan in Ashland, or going to family get-togethers, or just getting her out of the house. She kind of became a mother to her mother, really. It was a turnabout in roles. She spent a lot of her time taking care of Mother.

In Lori Ann's mind, though, she was just doing what you do—taking care of your mother when she needs you. What a wonderful and inspiring love she had for her mother to be willing to do that. They could have hired someone, but Lori Ann wasn't married, and she wanted to take the responsibility. She did have some good support from my brothers and daughters and all of the other cousins. They didn't live too far from Lori Ann and were there for her and her mother, too. The family would go over there a lot and do things together.

I think Lee and I have raised good children. Ray and Dean did, too. My brother Ray married a lovely woman named Lenora. They had four children together—Jack, Jim, Judy, and John. Ray died in 1994. Lenora passed in 2009.

When Dean was just twenty-one, he and Eleanora were married. Actually, nobody really called Eleanora by her Christian name; everybody called her Susie. Dean and Susie were married for fifteen years and had three children together by the time Susie passed away. Dean and Susie's son, Danny, is gone now, but I still have my two nieces—Sherilyn and Debbie.

When Dean was thirty-six, he met a woman named Rose whose husband had passed away. About a year later, Dean and Rose were married, and they stayed that way during the next thirty-five years until he died in 2003. They had quite a full house because Rose brought her five children into that relationship, and Dean already had three of his own.

Throughout the years, I began to realize that Dean's fatherly influence extended beyond the lives of his own children into the lives of young men in the community who needed mentoring. Ray Heimes, now president of Heimes Corp. in Omaha, told me that he and Dean had met over a business deal and Dean eventually became his mentor, helping him develop not only professionally but also spiritually. In fact, Ray said the best thing Dean ever shared with him was the Prayer of Jabez. Ray respected Dean for his ambition and energy—he called him a "walking power pack." That description fits. Dean taught him never to get into a comfort zone. Advice Ray said he never forgot.

At Dean's funeral, Ray Heimes said he felt grateful for all the time Dean had given him and appreciated how much like a father Dean was to him. At the service, Ray felt special until he looked around and saw men in front of him, behind him, next to him, all looking the same way he felt. It was then he realized the entire church was full of people Dean had made feel special, even parented, through his mentoring.

I'm proud of my brother and of his desire and ability to live his faith. As Ray Heimes said, "If you met Dean, you'd never, ever forget him."

Family ties have always been important to me and continue to be. My nine grandchildren and two great-grandchildren are the apples of my eye. My daughter Nancy and her husband, Dan, have two children—Matthew and Molly. Matt is very athletic and plays football for Nebraska Wesleyan and Molly works in merchandising. My daughter Mary and her husband, Kevin, have two sons and they both go to UNL. Alex is majoring in business and Austin is studying agriculture. Amy, their sister, teaches third grade in Elkhorn.

I'm so pleased that Suzanne and Wayne's son, Andy, is coming back to work for us at Sapp Bros. Petroleum. Abbi, his sister, is a full-time mom to my great-grandsons Griffin and Sawyer. Alison, Suzanne and Wayne's other daughter, is in Chicago working in public relations and advertising.

Bob and Cindy's little boy, Max, is six years old now. He's a joy and blessing to the whole family. When we all went down to Phoenix a few years ago, I even helped teach him how to swim.

Almost every one of our grandchildren has graduated from UNL, and I think that's terrific. All of them are such great people, I just couldn't be prouder of them. I am grateful for each and every one of them.

About those silver quarters and dimes Mother saved from the car wash money and gave to all of her children. I don't know what all the other brothers did with theirs, but I kept mine. Just this past year, though, I gave all of the coins to my grandchildren. I let them know that this was a gift from their great-grandma and great-grandpa and that these quarters and dimes were different from the ones they see today. They are a lot more valuable because they're made with real silver. The kids get that. They understand the value of coins, but more importantly, I think they understand the value of a loving family as the foundation for a happy and successful life.

Part VIII

Succeeding in Business: Lessons Learned

Whatsoever ye would that men should do to you,
do ye even so to them: for this is the law...
—Matthew 7:12

16

Prosperity and The Golden Rule: Lee Sapp

Throughout my career, I have been involved with many different businesses, both with and without my brothers. And I have enjoyed all of them, from the Sapp Bros. dealerships and other Sapp Bros. businesses to my own ventures in land investment, leasing, banking and insurance, and even coin collecting.

I believe the number one secret to success in business is to be honest, trustworthy, and sincere. If you have those qualities and know your customer comes first, you can't go wrong. If you were raised valuing those traits, which we were, it feels natural to take them into the business world with you. If we borrowed a neighbor's equipment while we were growing up, it was a law that we returned it in good or better condition than we got it. If you treat another person the way you want to be treated, everything should work out in the end.

Bill and I hope some young business people will learn from this book what it took us a lifetime to learn.

Lesson 1. Assess your capacity to own and operate a successful business. Unfortunately, just because you dream of succeeding at something does not mean your dream will come true. The dream to be a successful entrepreneur becomes reality for some folks, but not for others. Sometimes it's the economy that gets in the way. Sometimes it's lack of skill. Everyone can't be an excellent mechanic or airplane pilot or whatever he or she wants to be. We are all individuals. Just because someone's dad gives them some money doesn't mean that he or she has what it takes to succeed in business. God set it up this way, I believe. We all have different gifts and callings.

Lesson 2. Realize the lifeblood of any company is honesty, trust, and integrity. Treat people right and trusting them to do the same. It's the same old thing—so simple. But it works. I've done business with a lot of people who were smarter than me, but they knew they could trust me. I would show them my bottom line of, say, $1,000. And then I'd tell them, "I'm not going to sell this to you for what it costs me just 'cause I like you—I don't like you *that* much." That's what I'd tell them. I'd say, "I want $250, $300, or $400 on top of what I paid; otherwise, let's just shake hands, you go your way, and I'll go on my way." I'd show them the factory recap price. In fact, we'd just leave it on the cars. The invoice showed what we paid the factory for the car, and that's what I showed the customers. It always worked.

Because we were honest, people trusted us. Pretty soon we were securing all sorts of company car and truck accounts, like Kitty Clover, Fairmont Foods, Union Pacific, Kiewit, Hawkins. All the big businesses in Omaha bought from us because I started the policy that they could come in once a year and audit our files to see how much over invoice we sold their cars and trucks to them. They trusted me, though. I never did have one of them come down and audit us. Ever.

Honesty is just so important, and it's something we all get from God. And we brothers also got it from our family.

Dad was real big on honesty. The following story is an example of why integrity is so important in business.

The Seed

A successful Christian businessman was growing old and knew it was time to choose a successor to take over the business. Instead of choosing one of his directors or his children, he decided to do something different.

He called all the young executives in his company together. "It is time for me to step down and choose the next CEO," he said. "I have decided to choose one of you."

The young executives were shocked, but the boss continued. "I am going to give each one of you a seed today—a very special seed. I want you to plant the seed, water it, and come back here one year from today with what you have grown from the seed I have given you. I will then judge the plants that you bring, and the one I choose will be the next CEO."

One man, named Jim, was there that day and he, like the others, received a seed.

He went home and excitedly told his wife the story. She helped him get a pot, soil, and compost and he planted the seed.

Every day, he would water it and watch to see if it had grown. After about three weeks, some of the other executives began to talk about their seeds and the plants that were beginning to grow. Jim kept checking his seed, but nothing ever grew.

Three weeks, four weeks, five weeks went by, still nothing. By now, others were talking about their plants, but Jim didn't have a plant and he felt like a failure.

Six months went by—still nothing in Jim's pot. He just knew he had killed his seed. Everyone else had trees and tall plants, but he had nothing. Jim didn't say anything to his colleagues, however. He just kept watering and fertilizing the soil—he so wanted the seed to grow.

A year finally went by and all the young executives of the company brought their plants to the CEO for inspection. Jim told his wife that he wasn't going to take an empty pot. But she asked him to be honest about what happened.

Jim felt sick at his stomach. It was going to be the most embarrassing moment of his life, but he knew his wife was right.

He took his empty pot to the boardroom. When Jim arrived, he was amazed at the variety of plants grown by the other executives. They were beautiful—in all shapes and sizes. Jim put his empty pot on the floor and many of his colleagues laughed. A few felt sorry for him!

When the CEO arrived, he surveyed the room and greeted his young executives.

Jim just tried to hide in the back.

"My, what great plants, trees, and flowers you have grown," said the CEO.

"Today one of you will be appointed the next CEO!"

All of a sudden, the CEO spotted Jim at the back of the room with his empty pot. He ordered the financial director to bring him to the front.

Jim was terrified. He thought, "The CEO knows I'm a failure! Maybe he will have me fired!"

When Jim got to the front, the CEO asked him what had happened to his seed. Jim told him the story.

The CEO asked everyone to sit down except Jim. He looked at Jim, and then announced to the young executives, "Here is your next chief executive! His name is JIM!"

Jim couldn't believe it. Jim couldn't even grow his seed. How could he be the new CEO, the others asked?

Then the CEO said, "One year ago today, I gave everyone in this room a seed. I told you to take the seed, plant it, water it, and bring it back to me today. But I gave you all boiled seeds; they were dead—it was not possible for them to grow.

All of you, except Jim, have brought me trees and plants and flowers. "When you found that the seed would not grow, you substituted another seed for the one I gave you. Jim was the only one with the courage and honesty to bring me a pot with my seed in it. Therefore, he is the one who will be the new chief executive!"

If you plant honesty, you will reap trust.
If you plant goodness, you will reap friends.
If you plant humility, you will reap greatness.
If you plant perseverance, you will reap
    contentment.
If you plant consideration, you will reap
    perspective.
If you plant hard work, you will reap success.
If you plant forgiveness, you will reap
    reconciliation.
If you plant faith in Christ, you will reap a harvest.
So, be careful what you plant now;
    it will determine what you will reap later.

—Author Unknown

I actually know a couple of CEOs who have tried this exercise with their employees and had it turn out the same way. Some of the employees cheated.

Lesson 3. Do what you love. Don't go into business just for the money. If you're in it because of greed, you ain't going to make it. You've got to do what you enjoy. Many people have come to me saying, "I want to do this," but after I talk to them awhile, I ask them, "What's the number one thing you like more than anything else in the world?" And it's something totally different. My favorite thing to do is to meet people and sell. I love everything I do because there is really not much difference between getting a bank account and selling a car. If people like me and trust me, they come to me.

If I'm selling a car or truck, naturally price enters in on that sometimes. But I've had people say, "You've done me so many favors, Lee, I don't care what price you have on it" because they trusted me, and they knew I wouldn't cheat them. Building that kind of trust with customers is my passion.

Another passion of mine is collecting coins. Long ago, I had an old friend, Vern Elder, down in Kansas City I sold Snow Crop food to. He collected pennies and dimes and encouraged me to start saving them, too. I said, "That's the only kind of collection I can afford—pennies and dimes!" In time, I came to trust my friend, and he taught me what coins to buy. I started that back in '55, and I've been collecting silver and gold for more than fifty years now.

I've always bought gold, silver, and land because it's what I love to do. And it has just happened to pay off.

Lesson 4. Meet the needs of your community. There was only one bank in Ashland in the late 70s, when my son and I bought back the Ford dealership in town. When the Ashland folks came in to see us and buy their cars, a few of them asked us if we would build another bank in town. We had heard rumors the owner of the existing bank had gotten his own way all these years because the people had no other place to go. He had a monopoly.

I told the people from town that I didn't know anything about banking. But, I checked into it and talked to a few friends and some bankers. I had never had any experience before starting any of my other businesses, so I figured the golden rule could apply to banking, as well. If you're good and honest with people, they'll do business with you. That's always been my philosophy and the brothers' way of thinking, too, I believe. We already knew everybody in town, so we figured we already had their trust, at least we hoped so. So, I talked to banking experts to learn the simple banking rules and what the FDIC controls as well as what investment would be required of me.

I tried to lay the groundwork to succeed before opening the doors of the Ashland State Bank. One thing that helped was that most of the shareholders were townspeople. My brothers were not involved in this deal at all. I had the most money invested in the bank, but every stockholder and director had to buy a small amount of stock to be on the board. That way, they had a personal interest in the bank's success.

I really tried to determine the needs of the community and meet those needs. The other bank was closed for every holiday—major or not. We decided to close only on Easter, Christmas, and the big ones so that customers could do their banking with us when the other bank couldn't serve them. We wanted to be open when the competition was closed, see.

And it all worked out. On June 7, 1977, we opened Ashland State Bank in Ashland, Nebraska. I had a bank president, but I was hands-on with any money deals. The bank president or the vice president would take the deals in and then call me, and I'd go out there every day and check the paperwork and okay the loans. I was in charge of the bank and the final say-so, but I had good people working with me.

I'm sure the other bank in town was not happy with me, but competition is the American way. We were very successful. My bank turned a higher profit than any other one in the state of Nebraska at the time. The banking business went so well for me that later on I opened up another business—Sapp City Bank—near our truck stop on Interstate 80.

Although I really enjoyed the banking business, I got out of it in 1999 when Walter Scott and his family offered me a price I couldn't turn down. Now the old Sapp City Bank is called Centennial Bank; I do still own the building, though, and rent it to them. Last time I was in Centennial Bank, I noticed a big sign they had posted that told customers the bank would be closed on Columbus Day. I told them, "You guys ought to be open on holidays because your competition is closed. If people need to do some banking on Columbus Day, and you're open, then you will get their business." It worked for us.

I still participate in most of the Sapp Bros. deals. Bill and I are the only two brothers left, and I would say we are the two most aggressive ones, if you want to call it that. We try our best to be good managers because if you aren't a good manager, you aren't making any money. Working hard on something you love is the best thing you can do. I've done it nearly all of my life, and I have no regrets about that.

Lesson 5. Consider building a business with family members. The advantages of going into business with your family are teamwork, trust, and a similar work ethic and values. You don't have to be just like each other, though. In fact, it wouldn't be beneficial to have a family business if all people involved thought alike. You've got to have different ideas coming in. That's why we always voted. You're fortunate if you get people who think differently from one another and have different opinions. Otherwise, there are no new ideas, and that will cause more friction than good.

Lesson 6. You are no better than the people you hire. There is something called progression. If you hire the right people and listen to them, you will move forward. Your company is no better than the people you hire, see.

If you're running a good-sized business, you can't do it all yourself. If you don't have good employees to work with you, it's not going to work out. You need to know the background and values of your employees and find the most honest, respectful, trustworthy people you can. And people who truly have all of those qualities are going to be grateful to be working for a company that values those attributes, too. It's a good match—a win-win—and in our case, employees stick with us for decades, and we stick with them. It's hard to find people like that to do business with, and once you find them, you don't want to let them go. I can see that challenge coming up for us in the future.

I had the very best secretary in the world, Pat Balvanz. I hired her at the Snow Crop office in Kansas City, and she soon became an integral part of my business. She followed me up to Omaha when the brothers and I went into business together. Pat didn't work so much for Sapp Bros., though, as much as she did for me and my own private businesses. She simply didn't have time to give to Sapp Bros. because she was so busy with everything else. Naturally, she knew the brothers and they would call her if they were looking for me.

Pat was a workaholic, I'm telling you. She'd come and babysit with the kids and take care of the dog. Maybe she would have found another man and gotten remarried if she hadn't been working so hard for us. Maybe that's our fault. But we didn't ask her to do it; she just volunteered. She loved the work, my kids, and my wife. We all got along very well. Pat was with me so long, she was kind of like my family. And to this day, her son still buys cars from us.

I gave bank stock to her, as well as to some other people like our lawyer Fred Kestler, Harold Cooperman, owner of the No Frills Grocery Stores; and friends such as Harlan Nelson, who was an executive with Phillips 66 and a stockholder in my leasing company, and my son and daughter. I put their names on the bank's cornerstone.

Bruce and Lois Costra are another good example of loyal, long-term employees. They just had their fiftieth wedding anniversary not too long ago. Back in the day, he was a farm kid that came from somewhere north of Omaha. He became my very first Snow Crop truck driver in Omaha and then took care of the frozen food storage for me. Also from a farm, Lois was my bookkeeper in Omaha. And they ended up getting married. At their wedding anniversary party, I said, in jest of course, "My sales force was out working, but clearly there was some hanky-panky going on back at the office!" The whole place just roared. That's the kind of long-term relationship it's important to have with employees. So many of ours have been with us for a lifetime.

Lesson 7. Put sales first. You've got to have sales come first. If you don't have sales with a profit, you're not going to be around very long. It's not very hard to figure out.

Lesson 8. Make time to relax. Owning your own business can be extremely stressful because it takes an enormous amount of work. From time to time, make sure that you and your family get away from it all and find a way to relax together. You need to carve out time to enjoy yourself and your relationships with others. There is really no point in working your tail off if you can't enjoy your life.

Helene and I enjoyed spending time with our kids, playing cards, and going to movies. We went to a lot of movies. We also loved to travel. We visited Hawaii, Australia, New Zealand, China, as well as countries in Europe and South America, just to name a few places. We needed to get away sometimes from the stress of work and just enjoy each other.

My wife's favorite spot was Hawaii, so we went there twenty-two times. That's the love I have for her; she was something else. We'd fly to Maui, and then get on a ship. That way, we'd have to pack only once. We'd sleep on the ship at night and then get off and spend the day on a different island. We'd relax, have a real good time, and wouldn't do much. Even played golf a little. Oh, it was beautiful.

We also really enjoyed New Zealand and Australia because they were similar to the United States in a lot of ways. You could go for miles and miles and see nothing but bushes and trees and farms. And it was easy to understand people because they spoke British English there.

When Helene and I traveled to New Zealand, we stayed overnight with some sheep farmers and just had a wonderful trip. The wife even cooked for us. There were beautiful green mountains and very nice people. I bet that was forty years ago now.

Lesson 9. Be grateful for fringe benefits but remember what's really important. The brothers and I reaped some significant rewards from being in the business we were in and working so hard to get ahead. Throughout the years, we all won many trips from the car companies. I won a hunting trip to Africa back when Bill and I were running GMC. If you sold so many vehicles, you won a free trip. One year, we outsold Kansas City and gave GMC numbers they'd never seen before from this area. Many of the trips that Helene and I went on were gifts from the car companies.

I also won a couple of Rolex watches by selling Fords. One of them is even autographed to me with a copy of Henry Ford's signature on it.

To me, one of the best rewards, though, has been doing different deals with friends who trusted us and bought product from us—friends like Bob Devaney and Tom Osborne. Another is the satisfaction of seeing the Sapp tradition of family business carried on today through my son, Lee Alan. It has been a joy for the two of us to work together at the Ashland Ford dealership as a team for so many years.

Lesson 10. Treat your customers right and they'll treat you right. Building relationships with customers over time is important. It's not an overnight kind of thing. You can't stay in business as long as we have and not treat people right. Business owners who don't treat their customers well aren't in business very long. Luckily, I already had a lot of customer service experience before the brothers and I started our business. I had learned the importance of excellent customer service from my other jobs. And I guess I had some natural God-given ability, too.

We still have old customers who have been coming to our dealership since 1960. Their kids even buy from us now because we have built a solid and trusting relationship with their families throughout the years. And then those young people tell other folks they know to come. Word of mouth is still the best way to build a business.

My brothers and I came from near Filley and Virginia, Nebraska. When we bought our first truck stop in 1971, all sorts of people we had known growing up came up and bought from us. It seemed like they wanted to buy anything we were selling, actually. You would've thought we were having a family reunion when we opened that first truck stop. They were just so delighted to have us there and were so happy for us brothers. They were so happy, in fact, that they came up and bought gas, tires, and food from us. Many of them still do. We are very fortunate to have ties that go back that far and people who care about us. A lot of that older generation has passed on now, but we still have a lot of their relatives coming in.

Another example of building relationships over time is our mentoring of others everywhere we've lived. In some cases, we have been mentors for fifty years or longer now. I think that's about trust. Most people trust the Sapps because we tell it the way we see it.

Lesson 11. Learn from your mistakes and move on. What difference would it make if we sat around thinking about the business mistakes we made during the past fifty years? Don't ever go back over something you can't do anything about. It's simply a waste of time. Whatever went wrong, if you can't change it, just move on. That way, you won't obsess over the past. You will keep moving forward. I think that all of us brothers felt that if we made a mistake, we'd learn our lesson and move on.

Sure, we made some mistakes during the years, like hiring the wrong people every once in a while. Either the people misled us or we misjudged them—one or the other. But we learned as we went along. We'd have problems come up with employees, but we learned from every one of them. Each challenging situation had something new to teach.

Lesson 12. Who you are trumps what you sell. If you want to be a successful salesperson, you've got to be neat and clean, polite, nice, honest, and trustworthy. And you need to get a haircut.

Sales is not just about knowing the product line. It's about how people feel with you. If you're a jerk, even if you know your stuff and offer a lower price than the guy down the street, people are going to choose to buy from someone else that they feel comfortable with. If three car dealers have the same product, even if one of them is a hundred dollars higher than the others, people will buy from the person they trust.

Let's say hypothetically that we're a hundred bucks higher than the other two dealers. We have people who buy from us that say, "We could go to another dealer and get it for this amount." And then I say, "Are they going to take care of you if you have something go wrong?" And they say, "No, we want to buy from Sapp Bros."

And I do the same thing when I decide where to buy products. If I feel the salesperson is honest and sincere, even if he's a little higher, he's going to get my business. Excellent customer service is primary to your business success because of the trust factor. If people trust you and they know you're telling them the truth, why would they go anywhere else? I wouldn't.

Lesson 13. No matter how successful you are, you still need a mentor. John Promsky, our CPA, was a valued mentor of mine for many years. John taught me a lot about taxes and IRS deductibles. He always gave me good, solid information.

Jess Carraway was another mentor of mine. He's the Ford dealer who helped us get our first dealership. From him, I learned a lot about business in general and, specifically, how Ford worked.

Barry McCallan, the manager of Kraft Foods, also was invaluable to me. He had a lot more business experience than I did at the time and taught me a great deal. For example, he'd come down and rearrange the inventory and tell me why he was doing it a different way. He also taught me about merchandising—something else you need to understand if you are going to succeed in business.

Lesson 14. Try to own another business related to your own. Branching into the insurance field was very natural and easy for me. I got an insurance license myself because I realized that insurance is a big industry. In the banking business, we used to sell insurance, so that went through my company. Then when people bought cars at the dealership, the salesmen were instructed to sell insurance to them. Whenever it's possible to support your business by adding another that's related, consider doing it.

Lesson 15. Keep the faith. A lot of success in business seems to depend on the time and the economy of the country. But all real success comes down to having faith in God and trusting Him under all circumstances. I think that's all you really need to do to be successful, not only in business but throughout every part of your life.

∞------------∞

Nowadays, I help Lee Alan out with the Ashland dealership. I closed up my leasing company in November of 2008, so I am not writing up any new leases, but I still own several buildings. Because some of the leases are more than three or four years, though, I am collecting on some of them still. And I sell rural land out around the truck stop. Also, I'm on the boards of Sapp Bros. Petroleum and Travel Centers. It's all good. As for business lessons, I'm still learning them.

17

Experience, the Best Teacher: Bill Sapp

Fifty years ago, we started our business from absolute scratch. I had never been in the car business before, and I knew nothing about it. I didn't know anything about the truck stop business, either. So everything we learned was from experience—lessons from the school of hard knocks. I learned the bottom line is taking care of your customers and being innovative enough to come up with new ideas. Following are several of the many business lessons I've learned—mostly the hard way—during the past fifty years.

Lesson 1. Stick to your values. Throughout all our years in business, we have never lost sight of our values. Sapp bros. is about its people and what the company stands for: safety, attitude, pride, and professionalism.

Both personally and professionally, I always have tried to live by the words of the Golden Rule, "Do unto others as you would have them do unto you." When you're in business, most of the time you should feel that you truly are helping your customers. In fact, one of our slogans today is *Be Our Guest.* We treat our guests in a kind and respectful way, and I think that is how we all need to treat each other. At Sapp Bros., we are committed to excellent service and to treating every customer as our guest by providing a clean environment and quality products. We believe that there are six essential steps to treating customers as guests. First, we welcome them. Then, we use their names as much as possible. Brother Lee does a great job with that. Then, we take care of their needs, thank them, and invite them back. And we let them know the customer is really our boss.

Lesson 2. Meet your customers' needs. Just because we put the shingle up on our door doesn't mean that people started buying from us right away. Some of our early success was by God's grace, but it wasn't *just* that. We were hungry enough to discover what customers wanted and then driven enough to make it happen for them.

We did things for our customers that our competitors were not willing to do. As a result, our competitors lost a lot of business and we gained it. We were willing to go out there and meet our customers' needs, and that willingness was a big part of our doing as well as we did.

Being respectful of our customers and satisfying them is the main key to our success, especially out in rural areas. When a farmer calls us on Saturday or Sunday and wants a product, we'll have our men and trucks out there to help him out. That is what it's all about—filling an existing need in the community.

Lesson 3. Give customers a reason to choose your business over your competitors' by delivering an additional quality product. Buying gas and diesel is not an event that makes the average person exclaim, "Oh boy! I get to go down and fill up my gas tank today!" People just don't feel excited about that idea. But when they do need a tank of gas, they will think about where they want to go. Now maybe they decide to go where a particular brand of gasoline is sold because fuel does vary a little with different additives. But chances are that the customer won't just buy gas. We appreciate the ones that do, but we would like to give them another reason to visit us.

We're always looking for ways to find something that the customer wants to do while he's buying gas from us or another product that has appeal. For example, we encourage all of our travel center customers to pull up to our full-service pumps. Some do; some don't.

Now if you are in the Ogallala or Sidney, Nebraska, travel centers, you will see a sign posted that says, "Cleanest Restrooms in Nebraska." And they are. At those facilities, managers have staff go in to the restrooms every single hour to clean them. I have a big stack of letters from people writing to tell us how great our truck stops are because of our clean restrooms.

In Columbus, we have a sign that advertises "The Best Car Wash in Columbus." And we are, by far. Four years ago, we spent big bucks on that car wash at the truck stop. As the president of Sapp Bros. Petroleum, Bernie Raiter, says, we're willing to spend the dollars when we think it will pay off. At the Columbus car wash, we give a per-gallon discount on gas when customers buy a car wash in addition to their fuel. Month in and month out, that car wash does a great business. As far as fuel, when we first built it, we were pumping 60,000 to 70,000 gallons of gas per month. Just recently we pumped 190,000 gallons of gas there. And most of our increase in fuel sales is due to that car wash.

We are looking at putting similar car washes in our travel centers across Nebraska. When we first open a car wash, we create incentives to build up our clientele. At first, we give our customers a large discount per gallon on gas to encourage them to try the car wash. We want to get people in the habit of going there to use the car wash as well as to buy gas. Our customers always receive a discount from then on. The discount just comes right off at the pump. And you don't have to use the car wash that day. For a period of time, you can come back when it's more convenient and just punch in the numbers then.

So the car wash is one incentive for people to buy their fuel from us. They might reason, "My car's dirty; I need to wash it. They do a great job getting it clean at that car wash. I get a big discount, too, so I'll go there and wash my car." Often, people are lined up all day long, and they're there not to buy our gas. They want to get their cars washed!

Now in Nebraska City, we have the greatest little store. It has some real bargains to check out. People stop in just for that. And then in Salt Lake City, we have fast food at our travel center. As you can see, we really do try to give customers something else besides fuel to bring them into our travel centers—the cleanest restroom, the best car wash, the best store, the best fast food, the best restaurant. Something to give people a desire to keep coming in and doing business with us.

Lesson 4. Take a conservative approach. I'm a conservative. I will barter with you for pennies, just like I tried to bargain with my girls about those pearl rings. We all were raised that bartering was the thing to do. Every day, I am on both sides of the bartering fence. Some people try to talk me down, and then sometimes I'm the one who is deciding how far I can push a deal. I don't have any negative feelings about it. It's just business. I don't have a problem if anybody says "no" to my offer. It's my prerogative to ask and theirs to decline if they wish. Sometimes my wife is a little embarrassed by my bartering, though.

But a conservative outlook isn't just about trying to get the best deal. A conservative approach also needs to be applied to how much and what kind of inventory you choose to purchase. Purchase only the inventory that you believe you will sell easily.

Lesson 5. Maintain adequate cash flow. Cash flow is the sacred cow that affects your debt line. Look at cash flow as a safety valve. You can grow only to the extent of your cash flow. It's kind of like a farmer who rents a lot of land. It's great to have all that land so full of potential, but if you can't afford the big equipment and the seed and everything, it's not going to be very fruitful. He's got to have a banker or someone to loan him the money, or he won't make it.

Cash flow is a major problem that many entrepreneurs have. If they have a problem with cash flow and they don't solve it, it will drag them down in time. You have to have cash flow or you won't make it. Period. You cannot take on too much at once. That is a good lesson I learned over the years.

Lesson 6. Build on a transportation route. If you look at the story of Joseph in the Bible, you'll find that his trade route was along the established path used to carry merchandise by camel from point A to point B. Even the pyramids in Egypt were built along the Nile so that the Egyptians could float rock on big barges. As the world became more civilized, population centers developed near seaports. That's why you see a lot of major cities, such as London and New York, on the coasts. In the Midwest, towns like Nebraska City, Sioux City, Omaha, and Council Bluffs developed along the Missouri River. That way, produce could be transported from one point to another. Ships could come into the ports off of the Gulf of Mexico, as well. Waterways were how people brought merchandise in and shipped it out.

But then in the United States, the ships began to be replaced by the railroad. When the railroad tracks came along, communities developed near the depots, so they could get product more efficiently from one location to another. Chicago went through a huge period of growth once the rail centers were in place.

Even here in Nebraska you can see the effects of transportation on population growth. Back in the day, DeSoto Bend was more populated than Blair because DeSoto Bend was on the curve of the Missouri River. But then along came the railroad. It bypassed DeSoto Bend and stopped at a depot in Blair. As the years went by, Blair grew and DeSoto Bend got smaller.

Businesses built on transportation routes, like the interstate today, and on land located near them tend to become more lucrative more quickly than those located in other areas.

Lesson 7. Hire and retain good employees. One of the reasons that Sapp Bros. is where it is today is that we were able to find good people to work with us. In turn, we care about every employee and respect the experience each one brings to the job.

In business, having a good lawyer and a good accountant is imperative. We had both and that greatly helped us succeed. I think it's best to have good legal counsel who is not only an attorney, but also a friend who will be on your side. Someone that you understand and who understands you.

Ted Kessner was that someone for the Sapp Bros. He was our faithful attorney until the day he retired. Back in the day, he and I went to school together. He was graduating from the University of Nebraska Law College around the same time I was graduating from the University of Nebraska at Lincoln, and we worked at the *Journal Star* together, too. We were very good friends, and we—Sapp Bros. Ford Sales, Inc.—were his very first customer.

Occasionally, in business you run into some legal problems. When that happened, I would go to Ted, and he would either solve the problem right there or go to the right people to solve it. He did everything he could to help me and always acted in the best interest of our company. The few times that we got into problems we shouldn't have gotten into, he helped us out.

We did all of our business with him. When he retired, he recommended Bill Kutilek, but I still see Ted, and he still helps us push deals through. Ted was and is a real blessing to us.

A good accountant also is important because if you don't have all of the figures and don't know where you are financially, you aren't able to make informed business deci-sions. You need to have all of the facts first.

Our CFO, Allen Marsh, has been a real asset to Sapp Bros. Throughout the years, we all have worked with Allen at board meetings and have had some fun times. Of course, our meetings could be serious, too. We opened all our meet-ings with prayer, and Allen was a part of all of it. I think the grace of God was with us.

At Sapp Bros., we always have valued our employees. Most of our employees are trained very well. I have a college education, but a lot of our key people do not.

They've just been here a long time, are very observant, are good with people, and have quite a bit of on-the-job training. A lot of our employees in high-level positions started at the bottom and have worked their way up over the years. We are blessed to have so many employees who are honest, loyal, dependable, and offer important input. They are so easy to work with.

Some people wanted me to sell out a long time ago, but I said, "No, I don't want to. I've got a lot of good people here, and I want them to have jobs. I don't want to sell the business; I want them to run it when I leave." I'm sev-enty-eight, and I'm still doing what I've always done. I'm not going to quit working.

I even have a couple of very good, very loyal, retired employees I contract with from time to time on certain pro-jects. We pay them so much per hour now. They worked for us for thirty some years, and we know they are honest and trustworthy. That's why I like to hire them, even after they've retired. And I think they enjoy being back working with us.

Retirement can be a tough deal because all your life you learn information, go through training, follow your in-stincts, then it seems like it's all for naught when you retire. Some of our employees have bought and sold gas or helped us build things, but they are not going to use those skills in their retirement.

So when I call up these guys and ask them to do a job, they get really excited, jump right in, and get it done. I don't even have to give them any instruction. They just do the project.

Lesson 8. Work as a team. Common people working together can accomplish great things for their company or their family, even though they may not have extraordinary talent or ability on their own.

To work better together, we Sapp brothers created our own little democracy. We had to have harmony among ourselves to make it, and we knew it. The four of us made a policy that worked pretty well, and we used it for many years. If three of us felt fearlessly about going in one direction on a business decision, even though the three might be wrong, that's the way we went. If we discovered later that the fourth brother was right, then we would bend and go his way. If the vote was two and two, we wouldn't borrow any more money, buy anything, acquire any more land, or take any kind of action related to what we were considering.

We really didn't fight much. We all were important members of the Sapp team. On any solid team, you've got to have different personalities with different assets, and ours was no different. And that's good because if there's nobody with any ideas of what should or shouldn't be done, nothing will move forward. Some of us were more opinionated than others, and some were better peacemakers. You've got to have some people who are willing to step up and say, "Well, let's go and do this," or "That's crazy!" Maybe it is crazy, and maybe it is not, but you need that combination of people with drive and people with steadiness. It's like a good basketball team. Maybe one guy is better at hitting the hoops, but he relies on the other guys to pass the ball off. He needs the support of his teammates to make it work. And that's the kind of teamwork we had. Everybody provided input—some more strongly than others.

Long ago, we went to a bank and requested a loan for a considerable amount of money. The banker told us that we didn't have as much net worth as he would've liked, but the reason he felt secure in giving us the loan was that there were four of us. He figured that if one of us had a wife problem, or one of us decided to do something else or developed a drinking problem, that he would be able to get the debt repaid by the rest of us that hadn't gone astray. By getting four people to sign for the loan, even if one or two of us fell off the wagon, he would get his money. It turned out that none of us did, though. Everybody carried his weight. We were able to accomplish a lot and help our parents in their final days because we were all on the same page and worked together as a team.

Lesson 9. Solve your problems. Do not go into business if you can't solve problems. If problem solving is not your cup of tea, that's okay, but the business field is not for you. Sweeping problems under the carpet can be disastrous in the business arena. It may seem easier to think, "Well, I will let that one go," or "I'll deal with that one later." But unsolved problems can fester over time and eventually cripple an organization if they are left untreated.

I think good businesspeople are good problem solvers. They delegate responsibility to people who can handle the problem, or they, themselves, get involved in solving the problem. I have taken over companies and businesses where that wasn't happening. The owners were good people, but they had problems that they did not solve. As a result, their business floundered.

To discover the problems that are occurring in your business, it's important to have good communication with your employees. Monthly meetings can help give employees a venue to talk and clear the air. When I first started out, since I knew nothing about the truck stop business, all the managers and I met every week. We spent half an hour to an hour going over all of our problems and what we should do to solve them. Managers really should be called problem solvers, because that is what their job is all about.

Some problems are simply beyond anyone's control. Chalk those up to bad luck. No amount of problem solving can overcome really bad luck.

Run toward your problems rather than avoiding them or pretending that they're going to go away. I believe this is good advice for every part of life—your marriage, your job, your business.

Lesson 10. Develop a conflict resolution plan. Anyone who's decided to enter into a partnership needs a conflict resolution plan to use when the partners disagree. The plan should be clear and written down in black and white before you take any action involving your business. That way, after you get down the road and have a disagreement, you can fall back on your plan and work it out.

A good conflict resolution plan involves a mediator—a person you both feel comfortable telling your side of the story to and someone who you think will be fair. In a family business, this person might be an uncle, a dad, a relative, or maybe just a good friend of both of yours whose judgment you respect. The mediator will make the final decision for you when you and your partner disagree.

I have seen too many family businesses fail because they haven't had a plan in place. By the time they realize they need one, it's too late. I've observed people in family businesses who get mad because things aren't going their way. They stop speaking to each other, sue each other, and get a judge involved. Then everything goes south. Next thing you know, it's all done, and they are selling their business to go off to try something on their own. My brothers and I were blessed in that we were able to work together, even though we had differences of opinion many times. We just were able to work through them.

When we have employee conflict at Sapp Bros., one of us sits the two people having the problem down and says, "Now listen, fellas, you've got to work together. If you can't work together, you both have got to go, and we'll find two people who can work together. This bickering and fighting and saying nasty things has got to come to an end. And if it doesn't come to an end, then you will have to go find a job elsewhere."

At other times, we might bring the arguing employees in, sit them down, and tell them their behavior isn't tolerable. We listen to both sides of the story, come up with a solution, and then move forward.

If you just leave your employees out there fighting with each other, destroying employee morale, and you don't do anything, the initial problem gets bigger. You just cannot run a successful business amid conflict.

Lesson 11. Take care of business above all else. We learned early on that we had to take care of business first. You must be so totally committed to your business that you are willing to give everything you have to make it succeed. Don't be afraid to ask questions or to try new things. Your business is your golden goose. If the goose dies, you have no income. Above all else, you have to take care of your business. If you do, your business will take care of you.

I think a lot of young people today put themselves first. They drain their business and pretty soon the business doesn't have enough volume to make it. But that's not the work ethic we were raised with. When Ray and I got started in the car business in 1960, we took very low salaries, put in many long hours, and worked very hard. In fact, we probably made half of what we did in the insurance business with Prudential. At the dealership, we worked 6:00 A.M. to 9:00 P.M., six days a week.

But for me, it wasn't like, "Oh, I hate to get up and go to work today." It was just the opposite. I couldn't wait. We had so many exciting things going on at work. We traded for lots of cars at the dealership, then we'd take them to auction and sell them to help our cash flow because we didn't have a lot of money. We had two weeks to pay Ford Motor Company for their new cars. So, we'd put a date on them, sell them, and then pay Ford the next day.

Because we'd take the trade amount off the new car price, we ended up with a lot of money tied up in those used cars. Our assets mostly were equipment inventory, parts inventory, and used car inventory. We spent a lot of time cleaning up cars at night, then we'd take them to auction in the morning because we needed the money to pay Ford.

All of us helped out with cleaning up cars. We were pretty young, and we were used to cleaning up our own cars and everything else on the farm, so this was no problem for us at all. In those early years, we were the sales managers, the salesmen, the clean-up boys, and sometimes the mechanics. We literally did everything when we first started. We worked very hard, and, as a result, we did very well.

Lesson 12. Decide whether you want your business to experience normal or accelerated growth. If you plan to grow your business at a normal rate, you will want to focus on the basics: providing great customer service, hiring and retaining good employees, maintaining cash flow, and providing quality products or services.

At Sapp Bros., our growth depends on helping our employees reach their potential, hiring more people if needed, and using existing equipment and facilities to increase sales.

For your business to experience normal growth, goals and plans should be set yearly with monthly follow-through. Sometimes acquisitions or mergers can be a part of normal growth, but usually we consider those accelerated growth.

If you would like your business to grow more quickly, you may definitely want to consider a merger or acquisition. Mergers and acquisitions offer a variety of pluses, including more opportunities to grow, quicker growth, and more economical benefits.

If you choose to enter into a merger or an acquisition, be prepared to receive phone calls from other marketers, real estate agents, and other brokers. These contacts will give you an opportunity to consider a variety of different options. Be sure you look at each situation carefully. If you and another existing business can reach agreement, make sure you get something in writing as soon as possible. We had one oil jobber back out on us because someone else came along and offered him fifty thousand dollars more.

If you are considering acquiring an existing business, ask yourself the following questions:

1. Does the company have a good customer base that we can retain?
2. Does it have good employees who will stay?
3. Are there any environmental problems?
4. Is the equipment and real estate fairly priced (market value)?
5. Are inventories current?
6. Will they keep accounts receivables or make acceptable arrangements?
7. Do you have enough cash flow to handle the acquisition?
8. Does this fit in with the existing business and area?

If all of these questions can be answered satisfactorily, consider purchasing the business. If you are considering a merger with an existing business, you should ask yourself the same questions. Mergers can be very beneficial for many reasons:

1. Key people usually stay.
2. The customer base usually stays.
3. Borrowed money needed for an acquisition is not needed for a merger if an exchange of stock will

work. Restrictions for company protection should accompany this exchange.

4. Usually, consolidations of personnel and equipment can bring about more efficiency.
5. Equipment and real estate no longer needed can be sold or leased to increase cash flow.
6. Some of the management obtained from the merger can become key members of your staff. (Others who are not productive must go.)
7. Previous owners can accept your stock for stock and not have to pay income tax until they sell the stock.
8. Competition is usually reduced.

Lesson 13. Stay competitive. To really succeed in business, you've got to be hungry and stay hungry. And that means paying attention to your competition. With the travel centers, we develop in areas where we know we can do better than our competition. We usually guess right. If you can't beat your competition, purchase them or merge with them.

GMC helped us figure out ways to make our trucks extremely competitive; it was a big plus. The car business is very competitive anyway, but we had low overhead. As we got bigger and bigger and our overhead grew, we had to keep finding ways to stay on the cutting edge of the industry. By the grace of God, we've managed to stay competitive in the marketplace all of these years.

We are always willing to spend the money to buy bigger and newer trucks than our competition has. And we've never been shy about spending large sums, if they can be justified. That kind of thinking has really paid off for us. We make the initial investment and become the first ones on the scene to sell a certain vehicle. Now, eventually, our competition figures it out and copies us, but it usually takes them awhile to catch on. Our seven-axle tractor trailers are a good example of that.

Recently, I looked at a truck stop I'd like to purchase in a southern state. We are planning on building a huge, high-end car wash on site because three thousand apartments for servicemen are going up all around the truck stop. Now, most servicemen want a nice car or nice pickup, and they want to keep it clean. At our car wash, they can clean their car and everything else. We have our sights on building the same type of car wash in a couple of locations around Omaha, as well. It's this type of field research and thinking that keeps us competitive in today's market.

Lesson 14. Take calculated risks. Don't be afraid to try new things. Sure, do your research and figure out the practicalities, but take some risks here and there. Going into business with my brothers in 1960 was an enormous risk. None of us had much money. None of us really had business experience. We were all pretty young. Each of us scraped together his ten thousand dollars to start with. Together, we had only forty thousand dollars, but we went up to Ashland and made the snap decision to buy the dealership in Ashland from the man whose partner was dying of cancer. If we hadn't taken huge risks like that throughout the years, Sapp Bros. would not be the success that it has grown to be.

Lesson 15. Whether you get a little or a lot in life, take it and do well with it. Consider these words from the Bible:

> For it will be as when a man going on a journey called his servants and entrusted to them his property; to one he gave five talents, to another two, and to another one; to each according to his ability. Then he went away.
>
> He who had received the five talents went at once and traded with them; and he made five talents more.
>
> So, also, he who had the two talents made two talents more.

But he who had received the one talent went and dug in the ground and hid his master's money.

Now after a long time the master of those servants came and settled accounts with them. And he who had received the five talents came forward, bringing five talents more, saying, 'Master, you delivered to me five talents; here I have made five talents more.' His master said to him, 'Well done, good and faithful servant; you have been faithful over a little, I will set you over much; enter into the joy of your master.'

And he also who had the two talents came forward, saying, 'Master, you delivered to me two talents; here I have made two talents more.' His master said to him, 'Well done, good and faithful servant; you have been faithful over a little, I will set you over much; enter into the joy of your master.'

He also who had received the one talent came forward, saying, 'Master, I knew you to be a hard man, reaping where you did not sow, and gathering where you did not winnow; so I was afraid, and I went and hid your talent in the ground. Here you have what is yours.'

But his master answered him, 'You wicked and slothful servant! You knew that I reap where I have not sowed, and gather where I have not winnowed. Then you ought to have invested my money with the bankers, and at my coming I should have received what was my own with interest. So take the talent from him, and give it to him who has the ten talents. For to every one who has will more be given, and he will have abundance; but from him who has not, even what he has will be taken away. And cast the worthless servant into the outer darkness; there men will weep and gnash their teeth.'

Matthew 25:14-30
Revised Standard Version

It seems so unfair to us that the Bible says the servant who received one talent and did nothing with it should hand it over to the servant who had ten talents. The man who had ten had more than he needed. Why didn't he give the one talent to the man who had four?

But that wasn't what happened. According to the word of the Lord, he gave it to the person who had ten. Fair? I don't know. The only thing I do know is that I read a lot into the parable that maybe others don't. It took me a long time to understand it, but finally, I came to the conclusion that regardless of what we have, whether it's very little or a lot, we should not be envious of others who have more.

When I was in high school, I was so envious of the six-foot guys who could jump in the air and make a basket. I was a pretty short guy so when I jumped into the air, they crammed the ball right down my throat. I said, "Lord, why can't I be tall and do that?" The Lord had no comment. But as I grew older and as I got into business, I realized that I was supposed to take whatever God gave me and use it to the best of my ability. And that's all I was required to do.

You know, some people work real hard and do real well, and others do not. But you shouldn't be envious of someone who can do something that you cannot. Turning green with envy is bad for your health—mental and physical. So my philosophy of life is that I don't have to be envious of anyone to be happy with myself. What I need to do is take what talent God gave me and use it as best I can. That's all I can do.

Lesson 16. Find the silver lining behind every cloud. My mother always told us that every cloud has a silver lining.

She was a very positive person and I think her advice was good. So when you feel like you have failed at something, ask yourself, "What did I learn?" "How can I become a better person from this experience?"

In business, and in life in general, attitude is everything. One of my favorite poems is "Attitude," by Charles Swindoll:

Attitude

The longer I live, the more I realize the impact of attitude on life.

Attitude, to me, is more important than facts.

It is more important than the past, than education, than money, than circumstances, than failures, than successes, than what other people think or say or do.

It is more important than appearance, giftedness or skill.

It will make or break a company…a church…a home.

The remarkable thing is we have a choice every day regarding the attitude we will embrace for that day.

We cannot change our past.

We cannot change the fact that people will act in a certain way.

We cannot change the inevitable.

The only thing we can do is play on the one string we have.

And that is our attitude.

I am convinced that life is 10 percent what happens to me and 90 percent how I react to it. And so it is with you.

We are in charge of our Attitudes.

Looking back, I wouldn't change much. Because I am a praying person who asks God for guidance all the time, most of my life has turned out even better than I had imagined. When we ask God for something, we always want a "yes," but sometimes "no" is probably better for us. And sometimes there is no good answer. It's best to just accept a difficult situation, let it go, and move on. Be willing to keep a bright outlook, even when things appear darkest.

Part IX

Giving Ways

For what shall it profit a man,
if he shall gain the whole world,
and lose his own soul?
                    —*Mark 8:36*

18

There Is No Place Like Nebraska! Lee Sapp

When I was growing up, my family always said I'd give my overalls and shirt to anybody that needed it. That's just my nature, I guess. I didn't have much to give people while I was growing up—just little things maybe. But all of us brothers and sisters sure had the inclination to give to others.

I think we are all generous in part because our mother wouldn't let any guest leave our house empty-handed. If someone came over, that person was leaving with something. Sure, it may have amounted to nothin' but a hill of beans monetarily, but she wanted to give them something—either a slice of bread in their hands or a donut or a kolache. Something. Her mother was like that, too.

I've been very fortunate to have done as well in business as I have throughout my life. I'm a very lucky man. But when you die, you can't take your money with you, so I figure you might as well leave it here for people to enjoy. It's meant a lot to me to have the means to be able to give back to the community like I always wanted to growing up.

Now, Bill is very generous with his money, as well. He gives a lot of his money to churches and so forth. But I have focused more on donating to Nebraska universities and their athletic programs. I've been happy to contribute to nearly every college and university in the state of Nebraska. I think I've been drawn to give primarily to university athletic programs because I love sports. My brothers and I played them, my kids played them, and my grandchildren are playing them. We all attend a lot of Nebraska sporting events, and always have, but my personal favorite is Nebraska football. Helene and I would go to an early game down at UNL on a Saturday and then hurry home and change into our UNO shirts to go to a UNO game that evening. I've supported the UNL program by contributing in 1989 to a new recreation facility and to the UNO program by helping them build a new field house in 1998.

My connection with the University of Nebraska at Lincoln began back in 1962 when Bob Devaney came to Nebraska as football coach. See, when we got Bob Devaney, football at the University of Nebraska at Lincoln was at the bottom of the pit. That went for football in general all over the state. So we loaned him cars so that he could get out there and travel the state, get acquainted with people, and sell himself. And let me tell you, Bob Devaney was quite the character! He had a great personality, and people really liked him. He had a unique way of motivating people, and he could motivate anybody. And he turned Nebraska football around 180 degrees.

Later, I got acquainted with Tom Osborne, who became one of Nebraska's great football coaches; he liked me and I liked him. One time Tom had just bought a fishing boat because he loves going fishing, so I decided to furnish him with a new Ford pickup truck to pull his boat. Well, I'd belonged to Happy Hollow Country Club for years and years at that point, so at a party there in Tom's honor, I said, "I really don't know why Tom needed a boat for fishing because he's the only guy I know that can walk on water!"

Tom and I have been good friends for decades now. We talk on the phone, and he always helps me when I need it. He's a very good friend, and I think we both really value each other. I am so grateful for Tom.

In fact, Tom Osborne is my number one mentor, and there are a lot of good reasons I see him as that. First of all, he's a great leader. He has set a great example for youth and has helped so many kids with difficult backgrounds, like those with a history of using drugs or a tough family life. He has turned those kids around by teaching them values. At countless events honoring UNL's football players, I've seen boy after boy cross the stage to stand at the podium and say how tremendously Tom Osborne has influenced his life.

Tom has taught me through his Teammates program that mentoring is an important way to give back to the community. With his encouragement, I helped mentor a troubled kid for an entire year. At Ashland State Bank, people frequently came in to ask for money to start up their businesses. If they deserved the loan, I would give it to them, of course, but I also offered to mentor some of them. I helped several families get started in business that way.

Another reason Tom is my mentor is that he has helped me strengthen my relationship with God and my ability and willingness to pray. It seems to me that Tom has a very close relationship with the Lord.

Most of our donations have gone to either UNO or UNL, or other colleges or universities in Nebraska. I met my real good friend, Don Leahy, at UNO when he was the athletic director there back in 1974 when my son, an All Metro quarterback, got a scholarship to play football for UNO. Don started UNO's Maverick Club and made me treasurer. We had six dollars in the kitty. When my good friend Jack Lewis became my replacement years later, the Maverick Club was on more solid financial ground.

For thirty-six years, Don and I had the privilege of breaking bread either at breakfast or at lunch with some of the finest men in the city, friends of ours like Father Hupp from Boystown, UNO chancellors Ron Roskens and Del

Weber, head coaches Mike Denney and Pat Behrns, as well as businessmen Ron Kiger and Lyle Remde.

To this day, Don's still one of my best friends. Throughout the years, Helene and I had many wonderful times with Don and his wife, Carmen. I just gave Creighton University, where he also coached, the money to dedicate a Hall of Fame room and name it after him and his wife. He is a wonderful person.

Helene and I also thought it was important to help out the little Nebraska towns, like the ones we Sapps were raised in, so we built community centers and some other buildings in some small Nebraska towns such as Filley, Pawnee City, and Virginia. Other favorite projects have been helping fund the drive-through zoo out at Mahoney Park and supporting the Henry Doorly Zoo in Omaha.

Out of all the fourteen structures that Helene and I have funded across the state of Nebraska, I must admit I have one clear favorite. The one that's most meaningful to me is the Hurless and Emily Sapp Community Building with our parents' names on it in the town of Filley, Nebraska, where we grew up.

See, in 1999 I was traveling to see my sisters in Beatrice. On the way there, I ran into a banker in Filley, and he started telling me about the troubles his town was having. His main worry was getting a rural fire department to serve the farmers and everybody else in the community.

Later, I thought about our history in Filley, and I realized Helene and I could help. I said to the folks in the town, "Well, let's build a building!" And now they have their chamber of commerce and two fire engines housed there and also use it for square dancing and barbecues. They can go and put out any fire that starts now.

It's nice to have the opportunity to fund buildings in the little towns because their citizens are just so grateful. They haven't got the money to do things like that.

Several years ago, Bill and I each gave a hundred thousand dollars for a track at Ashland-Greenwood High School on behalf of our families and Sapp Bros. Our very first dealership was in Ashland, and that community has been very good to us, buying our cars or trucks, buying insurance from us, banking with us, purchasing propane or fuel from our petroleum company, or just stopping by our truck stop to eat or buy something. And this community support is still going strong today. What we did for the track at the Ashland-Greenwood High School was really from the community and the customers who have been good to us. The money just happened to pass from our hands to the school. The people of Ashland have always had our appreciation and thanks. In funding the track, our family was only showing the generosity shown to them by the people of Ashland throughout several decades.

Helene and I had the good fortune to be able to put eighty-four kids through college. See, I received a lot of letters and cards from kids telling me that their parents didn't have enough money to send them to school. And I knew how they felt. My mother and dad couldn't afford to send us to school, either. Of course, the fact that I still don't have a college education is my own damn fault. I used to think way back in the day that you couldn't get a good job if you didn't have a college degree. Today that's even truer, so I thought that giving away these scholarships would give kids a chance to become good businesspeople. And some of them did, and some of them didn't.

I remember there was a waitress who always used to wait on Helene and me. She couldn't afford to go to college, so we helped her out. We also helped out some of our son's friends who were having hard times or other people we just met along the way.

Later on, Athletic Director Don Leahy and UNO administrator Don Skeahan would interview the scholarship applicants for me, and then I would meet with the final applicants to decide who would receive the scholarships.

Most of the kids that were in the running were high school seniors. When I'd sit down with these kids, I would talk with them about their families—their moms and dads and their brothers and sisters—and try to learn what kind of people they were—their values and their work ethic. And, I'd see how their grades were.

The ones I awarded scholarships to would get the money right off the bat and were sponsored for four years until they graduated. Unless they had failing grades, that is. If they didn't get passing grades, the scholarship ended. So, they made their own way. They either got the grades or they didn't. But I do believe that every single one of those eighty-four kids graduated from college.

And all but one of those eighty-four scholarships were kept within the state of Nebraska. Most scholarship students went to UNO, although we supported students at all five state schools, including UNL, Chadron State, Wayne State, and Peru State. We also send students to Bellevue College or as it's now known, Bellevue University. Only one person went out of state to study and that was to Kansas. We felt good about keeping most of the money in Nebraska. That way, we reasoned and hoped, the kids who went to school around here would contribute to our economy by working in our state after their graduation.

What I didn't realize would happen was that these scholarship kids would go on to really help us. Because they were grateful to us for what we had done for them, they banked with me and they bought cars from me. I didn't anticipate that, but it turned out very well for all of us. We used to get a lot of cards from all those kids; it was kind of like we were family. But they've grown up now. Some have died, or they've got kids and are real busy now. But a lot of them still come and see me and even buy cars from Lee Alan.

I'm glad that I helped all those kids get through school. I mean, how could I have spent the money any better? I've always thought giving scholarships was a good idea.

Another passion of mine is funding a boys' wrestling program called the Westside Wrestling Club. A good friend of mine, Gene Barnhill, created that program to train boys to be excellent wrestlers. Gene was quite the wrestler himself, actually. He knew how to wrestle, and he wanted to help kids learn to enjoy the sport to keep them off the streets, build their self-esteem, and stay healthy. That's what motivated him to start the program originally, and it's just kept going and going.

I met Gene back in June of 1967 when he bought a brand new Ford pickup from me out at the Blair dealership. He's a house builder, and he eventually built the addition on my house. Gene's a wonderful man with a great wife named Sue. He's just an old Nebraska boy with good ways and good will. We've known him for a long, long time now. He buys his vehicles from Lee Alan now, but I remember selling to him back in the day.

Well, one day a long time ago, Gene and I were talking about his youth wrestling program. He wanted to add on to his building to accommodate more kids. That sounded like a great idea to me, so I was happy to help him get that done.

Gene's got a beautiful place for the boys to wrestle now. He's come a long way, too. Now he and his sons own a gym in Omaha called Better Bodies. And he stops by and sees me all the time. Gene even gave me a lifetime membership to his gym. He has coached many boys during the years, and a lot of them have gone on to be very successful. Gene's still at it—he's still helping kids.

Helene and I were not the only ones in the family who recognized the importance of giving to others. Lori Ann, my daughter, requested to have her money go into a foundation when she passed away, so we set up a trust fund in her name. Lori Ann's Foundation is overseen by her brother, Lee Alan, and her best friend, Pam. Lee Alan did most of the work to set it up. It's designed to help people going through hardship afford to go to college and get the things they might need while they are there.

Another population I feel strongly about supporting is World War II veterans. In sponsoring different events for them, I've gotten the chance to talk with a lot of vets, and those conversations have been very interesting to me. See, they'd been raised in the Depression era, like me, but they were a little bit older. The war ended the year I graduated from high school.

Those veterans told me what I had always believed—their going through the Depression helped us win that war. They all knew hard times, see. They didn't have anything. When we were growing up, if something broke, you had to find some way to fix it. There was no running down to the store and buying this or that.

For most of the vets, the military was a step up from what they were used to. They weren't worse off than before they joined; in fact, for many it was a better living than they had had at home. In the military, they received new shoes, new boots, new uniforms, and good food. A lot of people made fun of C-rationing, when, in fact, it was pretty good eating, comparatively. Now in the military you might get a little more discipline than you were used to, but the Army and Navy fed you pretty good.

Our military people were tougher than hell. They were born at the right time, and they grew up tough and deprived. So you put them overseas in a foxhole, and the enemy didn't have a chance. They had no idea how tough our people were.

Now all of this is just my take on the matter. People who know me, they all say the same thing. We don't always like to hear what you say, Sapp, but we understand what you're saying. But I did get the same story from pretty near every one of those vets I talked with. Tom Brokaw wrote a book called *The Greatest Generation* about the same thing. They were great patriots, and I'm proud to have known so many of them.

19

Going into All the World:
Bill Sapp

My wife once told me this story about God the Cowboy. In the story, all of us humans are horses and God is the Cowboy. One day the Cowboy comes up to a corral, and one of the horses goes over to let the Cowboy pet him. Other horses follow suit. Eventually, the Cowboy puts a bridle and saddle on one of the horses and then climbs on. The horse lets the Cowboy take charge of his life.

But there were other horses that would have no part of that. They wanted to do as they pleased. Sometimes they fought the Cowboy and tried to buck Him off. Some of them finally decided that the Cowboy wasn't so bad after all, and they allowed the Cowboy to take charge. They probably became some of His better horses.

If you apply that analogy to humans, it raises certain questions. Why is it that some people don't have a desire to accept Jesus Christ as their Lord and Savior, whereas some fight it but eventually do accept Him? I think all of us are somewhere in that story; we either accept Him or want nothing to do with Him. It's a decision that we all have to make.

I'm a committed Christian. I committed my life to Jesus Christ when I was eighteen years old, and I've always been interested in bringing others to know Him. But no one can accept the Lord for anybody else—everyone has to do it for himself or herself. I try to keep everything in proper perspective. If you try to push Christ on someone, the person will probably withdraw. I do my best to share my love of Jesus in a loving way. By sharing and witnessing, I believe we can stir another's interest and encourage him or her to learn more. That's what Jesus did. He went out in the world, reached out to people, and taught them how to live.

I've been a member of Gideons International for a number of years. It's an organization of Christian business- and professional men whose purpose is to distribute the word of God throughout the world. Their first places of distribution were hotels and motels; now the Gideons reach hospitals, nursing homes, prisons, and a number of other places. The Gideons bring the gospel to a wide audience—from U.S. servicemen to people in third-world countries to children on Mount Kilimanjaro and to many others.

I was privileged to go to Africa in 1989 with twenty-nine other Gideons. We traveled to Zimbabwe and to Tanzania. We passed out 343,000 Testaments to African children on that trip.

We woke up daily at 4:00 A.M. We'd pray and then meet the brothers from the other Gideon camps in the area. Then, with vehicles—usually Land Rovers—we would distribute Testaments each of the sixteen days we were there.

Each day, different brothers would travel a considerable distance from where we were staying to various tribal areas where the schools were. Usually, we would drive an hour or longer to get to the location.

One of the African Gideon members went to the schools beforehand to learn how many students attended each school so we would know how many Testaments to take with us. When we arrived at a school, the children would be lined up ready to receive their Testaments. We would talk with them about Jesus and what the Testament was about. In Tanzania, we had an interpreter help us communicate with the kids, but in Zimbabwe, the children spoke English. We would share that we felt Jesus loved us and them and that we were directed to tell the children that Jesus Christ is "the way, the truth, and the life, and no one goes to the Father except through [Him]" (John 14:6).

Toward the end of our time in Africa, the biggest miracle of our entire trip occurred. We were high on the Kilimanjaro mountainside. Most of the schools we'd visited had about 150 children.

On this particular day, we'd been out all day in a large Land Rover, and we were headed toward the last school of the day. You've got to understand that Kilimanjaro is one huge mountain and there's a lot of rain. There are banana trees and sugarcane and coffee beans, all brought there originally by the British. All kinds of vegetation are able to grow there because the snow on the top of the mountain thaws year-round, and then the water flows in streams down the mountainside.

Anyway, we walked up to this clearing and met the headmaster, and there in the clearing were a huge number of children. They filled up the entire field! I asked my driver, "Where did all these students come from?" He didn't know. So, we asked the headmaster, and he said kids from five or six different schools had walked as far as six miles down the mountainside to get to this clearing where they had heard we would be. They just showed up, hoping to get a Testament.

The original school we were supposed to be visiting had just an approximate date when we'd be there, and they certainly had no idea what time we would arrive. We couldn't give them an exact date because we had all the other schools to go to. If we didn't make it the day we had mentioned, then they could assume we'd probably be there the next morning.

But there they all were. They'd been sitting there all day long, just waiting for us to give them Testaments. I think we had around 175 Testaments left for that school, so we told everybody the situation—that we would give the school the Testaments we'd brought for them, but we didn't have any for the children from the other schools.

As I said those words to the crowd, an African Gideon pulled me aside and said, "Yesterday we went to a college that had closed down, so we have the Testaments we were going to give those students there. They're in the back of the vehicle." Then he leaned in and whispered, "I think there are about a thousand of them, Bill!"

So there we all were on Mount Kilimanjaro with no communication, no radio, no telephone, and no way to reach anybody. I didn't know if any of those Testaments were for somebody else or not. But, I thought, "Here we are halfway across the world on the side of this mountain with all these children that came down just for the Testaments." This was the only time during our sixteen days in Africa that we had such a large group of kids. I had no idea we had any extra Testaments with us. The people running the show didn't even know. The only one who knew was God. As far as I was concerned, God sent these children down there. So, we passed out over twelve hundred Testaments that day and nearly every one of those children got one.

I was amazed to see how God works each day in little things that we don't even think about. Maybe it doesn't seem like a big deal to a lot of people, but it was to me. That day was a beautiful, glorious demonstration of God's love.

Upon returning from Africa, I was asked to speak at different Gideon camps and to other groups about the trip.

Someone asked me if I could get his church group Testaments to take on a missionary trip. The Gideons have a policy that only Gideons can distribute their Testaments, but I said I would try to get some other Testaments for them to take. Now this opened up a whole new ministry for Lucille and me. Since then, we have purchased thousands of Testaments for people on missions, a majority going to Spanish-speaking countries.

Lucille and I both believe that it is very important to raise money, buy Testaments and Bibles, and pass them out in places where people can't afford them. According to the Bible, we all should help people: feed them when they are hungry, clothe them, take care of them when they are sick, and go see them when they're in jail. That's what Jesus taught. And when people asked him why, his response was, "If you've done it to the least of my brothers, you've done it unto me" (Matthew 25: 35-40).

There are so many places in this world where people are suffering. If you don't leave something behind to help them, the next year if you go back, their situation will be the same. Unless the word of God and morals and ethics get involved, nothing changes, so it's very important that the Word is delivered so people's lives can improve. You can find examples of Christianity helping countries prosper and make it on their own. The British took the word of God with them and the Spanish did not because their quest was for silver and gold.

My wife and I believe that passing out Bibles and Testaments is like sowing seeds. Some seeds are going to fall on the rocks, some are going to fall among thorns and be choked by them, but some will fall on good ground and grow and bring many to know Him.

Lucille and I had some interesting experiences when we traveled to Russia. We took several Bibles in our suitcases and decided that we'd just pass them out wherever we went.

While my wife and I were staying at a Kiev hotel, we were trying to figure out who we should give our Bibles to because we didn't have that many. Then we saw a beggar on the street, which was strange to see, because in Russia you just don't see many beggars. We observed him for a while, and pretty soon, a young person came along and put something in the beggar's cup. I turned to Lucille, and I said, "Now there is a man with a compassionate heart!" So, I went over to him, and I gave him a Bible. That's the way we chose who to give them to. I picked people like him.

Later on in Russia, we saw a bunch of ladies selling flowers on a corner. We tried talking to them, but we couldn't understand each other. One of the women seemed to be kind of a leader, so I tried to give her a Bible. Well, she didn't want it. She assumed I was trying to panhandle something, I think. I couldn't speak Russian, so I opened up the Russian-English Bible I had and let her read a passage. Once she figured out what it was, she was still dubious, thinking I was trying to trap her into something. I told her I was an American, and tried to use some gestures to communicate. Finally, she figured out that it was okay.

And then she wanted to give me all of her flowers! I didn't want any money or her flowers; I just wanted her to take the Bible. So I shook my head and said, "Oh, no, no!" and held my hands up. Finally, Lucille and I walked away, but she kept coming after us and coming after us. So then Lucille said to me, "Well, take some!" I took a small bouquet back to our hotel room. Once that woman figured out what was going on, she was not going to let me go without giving me something in return!

Throughout the years, Lucille and I have been fortunate to be able to distribute many Bibles and Testaments. To be able to share this journey with my wife has been very, very special.

One overlap between my spiritual pursuits and my business endeavors is passing out Testaments in the Sapp Bros. truck stops. Throughout our many years in business, we have given out more than forty-five thousand Testaments. Now, mind you, that's been over a lot of years. The Testaments are not in huge demand, but people do take them.

We pass out free Testaments at all of our truck stops. We put some in the chapels; otherwise, we put them in the truckers' lounge. We just have a sign with a symbol of a cross on it. The sign says, "Take one and see what Christ can do in your life." Some of the Testaments are in Spanish.

I don't tell many people this, but Grace University gave me an honorary doctorate in divinity. I think they did it because I went to Israel with them and tried to help them a lot. When people do find out about the degree, they say, "Oh, you're kidding!" and I say, "No, I'm not kidding!" If they are in my office, I add, "There's a copy of it right here. I have the original framed at home."

I am proud of my doctorate in divinity because it is based on my efforts to do good works as Jesus did. I have devoted much of my life to that cause. The Lord has been good to me. I couldn't have done it all without Him.

Part X

Looking Back, Looking Forward

*For God so loved the world, that he gave
his only begotten Son, that whosoever believeth
in him should not perish, but have everlasting life.*
                    —John 3:16

20

Gratitude for a Life of Good: Lee Sapp

I am working on retiring. I'll never make it, but I'm trying. The truth is that I will probably be working until the day I die. But my intentions are good. I'm down to just one secretary now who works at the truck stop. I have it in my head that I'll cut back on work, sell my house, and move to Tiburon, a local housing development, and play a lot of golf. But I'm not really sure what I'm thinking because I've always been active, and I still get up and go to work at 5:30 in the morning.

I do plan to travel some. Ray's son Jack is out in Wyoming, and he's always trying to get me to visit him. I may fly out to California to visit some good friends there or down to Arizona to visit some folks. But, you know, getting on an airplane isn't what it used to be. It's so complicated nowadays. They have to check this and search that. You have to take off your shoes and get patted down and go through the whole security thing. I know they need to do all of that checking now, but I'm not too fond of it.

When I look back on my childhood, I can see that just about everything I needed to know to succeed in business I learned early on. Our parents taught us that honesty is the most important thing. If we lied, we'd get the razor strap! So, honesty was ingrained in us from the time we were kids.

Conservatism was another important value instilled in us as kids. We learned not to buy anything unless we could afford it. And then there was the teamwork we learned growing up as brothers. We knew how to work together before we went into business. We trusted each other, and more importantly, we trusted God.

I believe my time in the military taught me a lot, too. In the service, we learned how to improvise because sometimes we didn't have much to work with. That ability to solve big problems with few resources was a big part of winning World War II, in my opinion. When we brothers brought what we had learned in the military to our new businesses, it greatly improved our chances for success.

Dad, too, taught us a lot. You know, he wasn't always real keen on our ideas, even when they were more efficient than his own. We brothers tried to get him to change his ways on the farm to more modern ones, but he usually wasn't very open to that. We learned how to listen to other people through those experiences because we knew what it felt like not to have our ideas heard. We've tried to listen to our employees throughout the years and show them respect. Just because we've succeeded in business doesn't mean we have all the answers. Nobody does.

I am grateful for all of the blessings God has granted me in my life. Helene and I enjoyed a beautiful life together. She loved me as much as I loved her. Although Helene wasn't raised in the Midwest, she and I were the same. We were honest with each other, and as a result, we trusted each other completely. We were married nearly fifty-five years by the time she passed away.

And our children! Everybody who knows me says, "How did you get two such winners for kids?" My brother

Bill will tell you how incredible Lee Alan is and how wonderful Lori Ann was, and so will our friends.

My advice for people wanting a fulfilling marriage is to have honesty and trust as the foundation of your relationship. Don't just think you're in love and rush into things.

I count my blessings every day in a prayer thanking God for being so good to me and my family. Material success comes and goes, but I always have been blessed with the intangibles—an abundance of integrity, fun, and love surrounding me. I had a great dad, a terrific mother, wonderful brothers and sisters, a devoted wife, and two shining stars for children. Now, I keep my family ties strong and watch my grandchildren grow into fine young men. I couldn't ask for anything more. I am truly blessed.

21

Gifts from God: Bill Sapp

My brothers and I really did come up through tough times. I don't think any of us ever forgot that; it just became a part of us. But every generation grows up differently. I know my daughters will never look at the world the same way I look at it, and I don't expect them to. My parents' view of life was different from their sons' much of the time. They often couldn't understand what we were doing and why we were doing it. But looking back, it all worked out just the way it was supposed to for everyone.

I really admired my dad in a lot of ways. He had a heart of gold and would give anything to anyone, although he didn't have much to give. He was very loving, but don't get me wrong—Dad was also a strict disciplinarian. He was the one who gave the spankings, but looking back, I think he was fair about it.

Big deals were hard to come by at my small high school in Lewiston, Nebraska. But according to the teacher who sponsored the Future Farmers of America Club, the trip the school had planned for us was going to be just that—a very big deal.

Students would take a bus to the huge American Royal Convention Center in Kansas City and spend a couple of days looking at the voc-ag exhibits and livestock judging. At night they'd sleep on cots, and almost all of these expenses would be covered by the school. A big deal, for sure! Only one catch: Each student had to pay for his or her own food during the trip. When I heard that, I had the strong feeling it would be a deal-breaker for me. Although I really wanted to go, I sure didn't have any money to pay for food. Knowing how tight money was, I could barely bring myself to tell my dad about the trip and my problem.

When I finally told Dad the situation, he didn't say anything. I remember it as if it were yesterday. I can see him pull his old leather billfold out of his back pocket and open it slowly. I glanced in it and saw just one wrinkled five-dollar bill. He looked hard at it and paused. Although he said nothing, in that moment I knew he was struggling with his desire to give me what I needed to make the Kansas City trip happen and with knowing how much he needed that five dollars to tide us over until his milk and egg money came in. Then he slowly pulled that five-dollar bill out and handed it to me.

I've never forgotten how Dad gave me all he had that day, an example of his generosity and love. And the trip? It *was* a big deal—all the way around.

Dad loved my mother very much and was a good husband. He tried to the best of his ability to fulfill that role with her and to be the best father to us kids that he could be. He did have a hard time trying to support a large family with no job and no money, but at least he stayed the course. You know, a lot of men of the Depression era just up and left their wives and children when times got tough. All over the United States, the railroad cars were full of bums who had just taken off and left a family behind. Some of them even committed suicide. But Dad wasn't like them. He was committed to my mother and to his kids and did the very best he could. I think we all understood that. I don't think there was anybody that felt that Dad wasn't doing his very best for us.

To succeed, you have to want to succeed. It's just sort of a human drive that people either have or don't have. But you have to keep fueling that drive and not give up. It's a constant struggle. In a way, I am grateful that I was raised during the Depression because I kind of enjoy a good struggle.

Looking back on all our years in business, I can see some essential elements that contributed to our eventual success. Our number one asset was that we learned back on the farm to work together as a team. That lesson was really a blessing because when the four of us went into business, we already knew how to work well together.

The second key to our success was growing businesses along transportation routes, namely the interstate. Any land along the major interstate exits is worth a great deal more than land in most other places. Maybe it's farmland when you buy it, but ten or twenty years down the line, it most likely is going to support some kind of commerce. My brothers and I were aware of this, and that is why we chose to buy fifty-two acres along Interstate 80 and Highway 50, originally to support a GMC dealership. Just recently we purchased forty acres of property along the interstate and have high hopes for its development.

I told Lee one time that we probably could have made a lot more money with a lot less sweat and tears if we just would have bought ten prime land locations along the Nebraska interstate back in 1960. Had we done that, we probably would've made as much money from the land as we made from our businesses. I am telling you that there are always opportunities to make money where the commerce routes are. Now, the means of transportation may change form in the future, but the land near the transportation hubs always will be a good investment.

◦------------◦

I'm happy to say the future looks bright for the Sapp Bros. For example, with expanding in mind, we bought land adjacent to the truck stop in Junction City, Kansas, to build a car wash there. A sizable discount on gas with a car wash can bring in lots more business and help the restaurant and store.

As of October 1, 2010, Sapp Petroleum and Travel Centers will form a new corporation called Sapp Bros. Inc., and each will be a subdivision of the new entity. My reason for doing this is that I believe the future belongs to organizations that run lean and mean and have enough cash flow to continue to grow. By coming together as one unit, the cash flow of each corporation will become one fund.

As Sapp Bros. Inc., we will experience significant savings on several fronts. For example, with its umbrella coverage for liability, the new corporation will save fifty thousand dollars a year by joining the two policies. Also, our IT departments will be able to function as one, saving us money when buying and replacing hardware equipment. Another example of cost benefit will be based on our large volume; adding petroleum and travel centers purchases together will help our buying power.

So, again, it's back to teamwork. These days, I have over a thousand people who work indirectly for me through the travel centers and Sapp Bros. Petroleum. The companies' successes are not so much because of me, but because of the people around me who have been dedicated to making our company grow and prosper. And to think we started with just the four of us brothers.

◦------------◦

At my age, I am not planning on doing a whole lot of traveling anymore. Now Lucille and I are more focused on sending out Testaments.

We did pass out seventy thousand Testaments last year, which included fifteen thousand to the Sudanese through Kevin McDonald, a pastor at Covenant Presbyterian Church in Omaha. A Sudanese doctor in the congregation encouraged the church to send Testaments to Sudan, and the church formed a committee to discuss how they might get the books to Africa. Lucille and I contributed the Testaments, and I helped them get the shipping containers. The books and tons of clothing and medical supplies left the church parking lot in November of 2008 and arrived at their destination February of 2009.

Spiritual outreach is very important to me still. I'm a solid disciple of Jesus Christ, and I'm committed to bringing people to know Him in the best and kindest way I can. But it has nothing to do with Sapp Bros. Above and beyond all else is my personal ministry. Serving the Lord is primary in my life. Being successful in my business endeavors is secondary. I put Jesus Christ first, because when it's all done and they throw dirt on your coffin when you're in the ground, it isn't really about what you've done for yourself; it's what you've done for others. I really believe that's more important than what I do for Bill Sapp.

If you haven't accepted Christ as your Lord and Savior, let Him have control over your life. I guarantee you will be better for it.

I want my grandchildren and my great-grandchildren to remember a couple of simple things about me. First, I'm a person who's committed to Jesus Christ. I'm a born-again believer. And second, I want them to know that I'm a team player, that I was able to work with my brothers all those years. It's not that we didn't have some problems, but we made it work. And it worked because their grandfather or great-grandfather had some great brothers who cooperated enough to make it work in the free-enterprise system. And those two things—Jesus Christ and being a team player—are really all they need to lean on. They need to find a relationship with Jesus Christ, but to make it all work, they need to pull together.

Acknowledgments

My most sincere thank-you to my friends and customers. Without you, my life as I have known it wouldn't have been possible. In the list that follows, if I have inadvertently left out anyone who should be mentioned, I apologize. This list is long and it's possible that a few names have slipped my mind. If so, please know that I appreciate all of you who have helped my brothers and me along the way.

Governor David Heineman and First Lady Sally Ganem, Joe Havicka, Scott Hazelridge, Jerry and Ruth Huber, Gary Judd, Rich Jensen, Cliff and Joan Jacoby, Bryce Johnson, Kenny Knight, Bob Kruger, Don Leahy, George W. Madsen, Jeff and Deb Schneider and Family, John Adkins, Jim King, Anne and Dianne La Barra, Karen Menard at Millard Roadhouse, Charlie McBride, John and Sara Murrel, Allen and Jane Marsh, Barry and Rita McCallan, Paul Meyers, Ron Blumkin, Henry Neff, Dave Nabity, Joe Newhouse, Les Perryman, John and Lynn Muller.

John Pribramsky, Jack Pierce, Lee Polick, Bruce Rasmussen, Allan Stein, Walter Scott, David Sokol, David Scott, Eugene, Ilma, and Alan Gottula, Don Skeahan, Don Bartels, Bob Sudder, Rich James, John and Jan Christianson, Todd Remmereid, Diane Gillespie, Bob and Dolly Welsheimer, Tom Hastings, David Johnson, Joe Daniels, Stan Daniels, Clay Rogers, John Neff, Trev and Angela Alberts, John

Sorrell, Allen and Linda Beerman, Clarence Werner, Harlan and Josephine Nelson, Charles DiDonato, Randall and Jane Smith. Mary Ann Steinrauf, John and Kathy Buchanan, Dan Novacek.

Dave Walker, Bruce Rodman, Dick Upah, Jerry Tegtmeir, Dean Thorburg, Bob Curttright, Shorty Morris, Bruce and Lois Costar, all employees at Centennial and Ashland State Banks, Dr. Jim Morgan, Rod Bates, Doug Buchanan, Bobby Smith, Lloyd Woodworth, Mark Zack, Gary Drake, Phil Dawson, Bill Danenhauer, Duane King, Howard Long, Tommie Frazier, Terry Fairfield, Jerry Gray, Jim Gerking, Ron Grebe, Rev. Jim Hardee, Rev. David Hanyes, Dan and Nancy Kuhl and Family, Dick Knight, Bill Krummel, John McCarthy, all employees of Whiskey Run Creek Winery, Frank Marelle, Officer Kevin Bridges, all employees of Lee Sapp Ford, all employees of Sapp Bros. Travel Centers and Petroleum, all employees of Calls for Less Telephone Company, Gene Barnhill, Dr. Lee Simmons, Wood Wright, Kelly Wills, Jeff Kellogg, Craig Swerizek, Jason Fett, Ted Kessner, George and Bonnie Dennis, Mark and Sheri Ladenburger, Connie and Sylvia Clausen, Clayton Anderson, Dean Blais, Martin Massengale, and Bob and Colleen Billings.

A special note of gratitude for Pat Balvanz, my devoted administrative assistant, for her thirty-eight years of outstanding support, and to Dawn Hansen, Pat's assistant, who has worked with me for twenty-seven years and counting.

Heartfelt thanks to gifted cancer specialist Dr. David Silverberg, whom I have known since 2004; to Dr. Jack Lewis, my doctor since 1982; and to Dr. Jack Belitz, my dentist since 1979. I owe my life to their skills and treatment. Thanks to the expertise and dedication of Drs. Silverberg and Lewis, I am a cancer survivor. With God's help, today I am a healthy octogenarian. I am grateful for their years of excellent care.

A very special thank you to Tom Osborne, who was kind enough to write the foreword to this book. He has been a very good friend for forty years and is one of the most honest and trustworthy men I have ever known. Living a life of integrity in action, Tom never speaks unless it is to benefit another person. He doesn't swear or belittle others; instead, he encourages those around him to always take the high road, no matter what the circumstances. I learn from his ethical and kind example and am honored to call him friend.

—Lee Sapp

With much gratitude, I thank my brothers and sisters; my wife, Lucille; our children; and Keith Hayes, who led me to accept Jesus Christ. I am grateful for Ted Kessner, our lawyer, and the many faithful co-workers, especially Bernie Raiter, Scott Brown, Bob Poland, Don Quinn, and Allen Marsh, all of whom had great input on our many decisions.

—Bill Sapp

Finally, we thank our friends, relatives, and employees for encouraging us to write the story of the Sapp brothers and for helping us recall the various events and experiences so instrumental in shaping our lives and our careers.

We express special appreciation to our editor, Susan Adams. During the many interviews we had with Susan, she asked us thought-provoking questions that made us stop and reflect on our lives—our successes and joys as well as our losses and sorrows. We appreciate Susan's skill in drawing out our stories and putting them on paper. It's been quite a journey.

Finally, we also thank publisher Rod Colvin and his staff at Addicus Books for their professionalism, expertise, and attention to detail in producing our book.

Sapp Family Tree

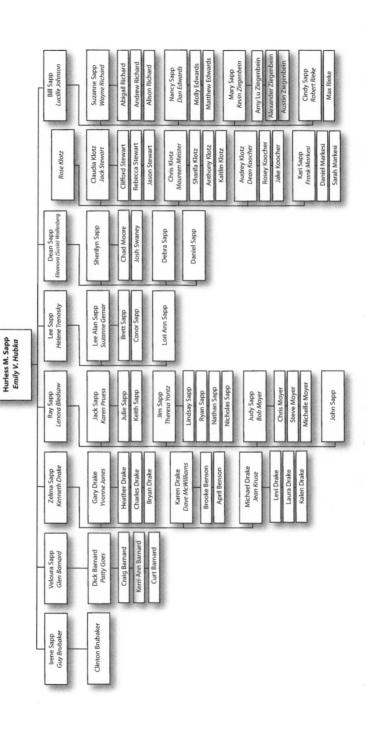

For Additional Copies...

Three Easy Ways to Order:

1. **Online orders:** www.AddicusBooks.com

2. **Toll free orders:** (800) 352-2873

3. **Mail orders to:** Addicus Books
    P.O. Box 45327 – Omaha, NE 68145

Please send:

_____ copies of *The Sapp Brothers' Story*

at $19.95 each: Total: _____

Shipping & Handling

$5.00 for first book   _____

$1.20 for each additional book   _____

Total Enclosed: _____

Ship to:

Your Name _____

Address _____

City_____State _____Zip _____

Personal checks, credit cards, or money orders accepted.

❏ Visa ❏ Mastercard ❏ American Express ❏ Discover

Credit card number _____

Expiration Date _____

Bulk Orders. Discounts on quantity purchases are available starting at 24 copies. Contact the Special Sales department at: **402-330-7493**